D1633810

THE POWER
OF MEDITATION

ENERGIZE THE MIND &

RESTORE THE BODY

LYIT
LIBRARY
LETTERKENNY

by **Christopher Titmuss**
photographs by **Rob Mitchell**

APPLE

A QUARTO BOOK

Library of Congress Cataloging-in-Publication Data is available upon request.

Published by The Apple Press
6 Blundell Street
London N7 9BH

Copyright © 1999 Quarto Publishing plc

All rights reserved. No part of this publication may be reproduced, stored in a retrieval system, or transmitted in any form or by any means, electronic, mechanical, photocopying, recording or otherwise, without the permission of the copyright holder.

This book was designed and produced by
Quarto Publishing plc
6 Blundell Street
London N7 9BH

Project Editor	*Marnie Haslam*
Editor	*Alison Leach*
Art Editor	*Elizabeth Healey*
Designer	*James Hitchens*
Photographer	*Rob Mitchell*
Photographer's assistant	*Gareth Sambidge*
Illustrator	*Chen L'ing*
Photographic Manipulation	*Mark Hitchens (pages 54-55)*
Art Director	*Moira Clinch*

QUAR.MHK

Manufactured in Singapore by Universal Graphic Pte Ltd.
Printed in China by Leefung-Asco Printers Ltd

ISBN 1 84092 178 1

contents

Why Meditate?

Meditation has an extraordinary power: the power to transform our lives. It is a way of finding direct access to the depths of ourselves, and to understanding our inner lives. It gives us the potential to transform misery, conflict, and neurosis. Through meditation we attend to our feelings, thoughts, perceptions, body, health, energy, awareness, and range of experiences. Meditation can be applied to every single moment of the day. It belongs to daily life as much as eating a meal or going to the bathroom. It is not confined to a particular posture.

Meditation is to be mindful
Each moment we are mindful is a moment of meditation.

MY INTENTION WITH this book is to offer people a wealth of beneficial meditation practices and exercises to serve their daily needs. If applied, the practices contribute not only to healing and health in the body, happiness and contentment in the mind, but also to extraordinary joy and insights into what authentic living is all about. We can uncover some of the troublesome layers in ourselves. We can investigate difficult aspects of our personality and realize a profound and liberating wisdom in life.

It is not uncommon for beginners to think that all meditation is much the same and leads to the same goal. This outlook creates a serious misunderstanding. Just as physicians use a variety of medicines to alleviate sickness, so the same principle applies to meditation. We use a range of methods to resolve various problems and difficulties. There are meditations for mindfulness, calmness, insight, and realization. There are meditations to generate energy, healing, and happiness. There are meditations to disperse suffering, overcome abuse, and deal with stress. There are meditations for the heart to enable practitioners to develop love and compassion. There are meditations to cultivate peace, contentment, harmony, and access to enlightening spiritual experiences.

The Venerable Maha Ghosananda, the patriarch of Cambodia, has been nominated for the Nobel Peace Prize four times, and has spent many years deeply engaged in meditation. He is regarded as a loving and saintly man. He makes long, dangerous walks across Cambodia to restore unity and peace to this troubled land, where there are four million antipersonnel mines in the ground. We had once been in the same monastery. In 1997, I stood with him on the steps of Capitol Hill, Washington, DC at the launch of the campaign to ban such mines.

The world's media were gathered there to report on the demonstration to show international support for the campaign. They asked him to express his view.

He came very quietly and mindfully to the microphone and said: "The landmines in the ground start from the landmines in our mind. We must uproot the landmines in our own mind as well." He then quietly returned to his sitting meditation on the steps of Capitol Hill.

I have arranged this book in a series of themes, as you may wish to draw on particular meditations to suit a particular need. But there is one meditation that applies throughout: mindfulness of breathing. It is important that you develop this as fully as possible, since it serves as a preparation for all the other meditations. What I suggest is that you first read the book from cover to cover. If one chapter is particularly relevant to your circumstances, then concentrate on it—having familiarized yourself in all

Concentration
A feature of meditation practice is a relaxed focus with single-pointed concentration.

the preliminary exercises of the four postures (see Chapter 2: Getting Started).

Alternatively, you may wish to begin with Chapter 2: Getting Started and systematically follow the instructions and practices from one chapter to the next over a period of several weeks, months, or longer. This will enable you to become familiar with the range of different practices. Later, you may want to specialize in one, two, or three meditations that are suitable for your own particular needs and development. I have noticed that in thirty years of meditation, I concentrate on three meditations: namely, mindfulness of breathing, observation of arising and passing of thoughts, and choiceless awareness.

The basic preliminary meditation practice throughout this book is mindfulness of breathing, probably the most extensively used of all meditations.

Meditation: Mindfulness of Breathing

It brings a wide range of benefits from stress reduction to energizing the mind, focusing the attention, and deepening awareness. Even though this book describes many different kinds of meditations,
I suggest you use this one first to get centered, then develop one of the others. The Buddha taught meditation as the direct route to enlightenment.
He once said that mindfulness of breathing was the finest meditation of all since it produced such a diversity of different benefits for the practitioner.

What does the word "meditation" mean in this book?

I give the word a very broad range of meanings. There are many terms in the English language that convey the spirit and meaning of meditation.

They include:

- *Being conscious of*
- *Being receptive to*
- *Being here and now*
- *Being grounded*
- *Being mindful*
- *Being connected*
- *Being centered*
- *Being focused*
- *Having single-pointed concentration*
- *Having choiceless awareness*
- *Having clarity*
- *Having moment-to-moment attention.*

How much time should I give to formal meditation?

THIS VARIES FROM person to person. What is important is that your formal practice is regular once a day, twice a day, every other day, or two or three times a week. Begin with the sitting posture for a minimum period of 15 minutes. Relaxing the body contributes to a relaxed mind. As you develop your practice, you may expand your sitting time up to 45 minutes per session, or an hour. Regular meditation every week is the key to widespread benefits.

Minimum

Expand your time

Can I do too much meditation?

MEDITATION CONTRIBUTES significantly to a deep sense of well-being. Meditation itself is not a problem nor does it create problems. It is a wonderful aid to resolving the problems of daily life.

Nevertheless, there are areas to be mindful of so that you do not put your mind under too much pressure in the name of meditation. If your body trembles or shakes in sitting or standing, then change to movement and dance. If experiencing doubt or finding yourself with questions that need answering, find an experienced meditation teacher, authorized in a long-standing tradition (see addresses on page 110).

PRACTICE

- *Not clinging to a single posture*
- *Not clinging exclusively to a single technique*
- *Not placing pressure upon yourself to achieve particular results*
- *Not using willpower, or forcing the mind to stay single-pointed*
- *Being mindful of becoming intense about meditation.*

I have attempted to explore the many opportunities for meditation in daily life. Like most of you, I have a varied and demanding workload that fills my days with many challenging tasks. Naturally, I draw a lot upon my experience of meditation to cope with my responsibilities.

That is why this book is a genuinely practical guide to combating the stress of everyday life.

Meditation is an alternative

WE SOMETIMES WONDER what is happening to our lives. We find the days, weeks, months, and years go by alarmingly quickly. Each year, it seems, passes more quickly than the previous one. Part of the reason for this is the constant feeling that we do not have enough time to do everything we want to do. We are obsessed with time and getting things done. We might wake up in the morning to a long list of tasks to complete. We find ourselves thinking of all the things that we have not done, all the things that we have to do, and how long it will take to do them.

There seems to be no place for real rest for our mind and body. It is not surprising that frequently we get home from work or study and flop in front of the television. On average we watch more than 20 hours of television each week, equivalent to nearly a day a week. It seems that our lives move between work, study, shopping, socializing, television, and sleep. Very occasionally we might

Time
Let us find time for formal meditation in our daily life.

speak of higher values, of deeper things. Few people seem interested in exploring together deep issues around living. We may feel inspired by what others do, and their contribution to existence, but it may not really affect us.

Traditionally, conventional religion has provided an important resource. It gives people the opportunity for prayer and reflection. But many religions are experiencing a significant decline in worshippers due to the incompatibility of religious beliefs with secular culture. But more and more people are seeking to find inner resources that are meaningful and practical in daily life. This is where the application of meditation comes in. Meditation is an alternative. It is not limited, not defined by any religious belief, nor does it demand the expense counselling would incur. Yet, it is certainly an invaluable resource in the pursuit of inner contentment and peace of mind.

We need to reflect on what areas of our life we would like to cultivate, and develop so that we can discover some of the benefits that meditation can provide.

What is my motivation to meditate?

Ten reasons

1 To overcome stress
2 To energize the mind
3 To open the heart
4 To develop focused attention
5 To find peace and contentment within
6 To dissolve unhealthy habits, addictions, and preoccupations
7 To heal old wounds and hurts
8 To overcome sickness and pain
9 To experience the depths of the inner life and our relationship to existence
10 To enlighten and liberate our life.

Ten benefits

1 Finding inner joy
2 Knowing ourselves better
3 Focussing on noble priorities
4 Generating love and compassion
5 Finding insight and wisdom
6 Dealing with difficult situations with clarity and equanimity
7 Embracing the processes of life from birth to death
8 Overcoming greed, selfishness, negativity, and worry
9 Feeling intimacy and closeness with ourselves, and life itself
10 Exploring spiritual experience and realizing the joy of a free and awakened life.

Nature
Contact with nature contributes to a deep intimacy with existence.

Will meditation relax me?

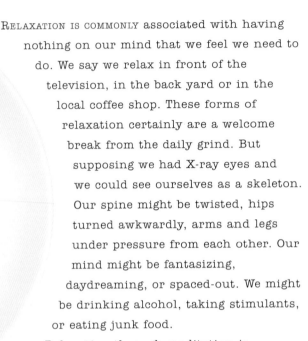

RELAXATION IS COMMONLY associated with having nothing on our mind that we feel we need to do. We say we relax in front of the television, in the back yard or in the local coffee shop. These forms of relaxation certainly are a welcome break from the daily grind. But supposing we had X-ray eyes and we could see ourselves as a skeleton. Our spine might be twisted, hips turned awkwardly, arms and legs under pressure from each other. Our mind might be fantasizing, daydreaming, or spaced-out. We might be drinking alcohol, taking stimulants, or eating junk food.

Relaxation through meditation is different. In meditation we turn our attention to our whole being, using the power of our mind to relax our whole being. We can do this in a wide variety of places and circumstances.

Sitting
The many hours you spend sitting daily can provide you with an opportunity to develop calm, inner peace through regular care to posture and breathing.

Coffee Break
Sometimes the benefit of a cup of coffee or tea can seem short-lived.

SIMPLE EXERCISE

1 Put the book down on your lap.

2 Straighten your back.

3 Stay still for 3 minutes.

4 Breathe in and out gently while feeling the presence of your body.

5 While staying upright, let your body relax.

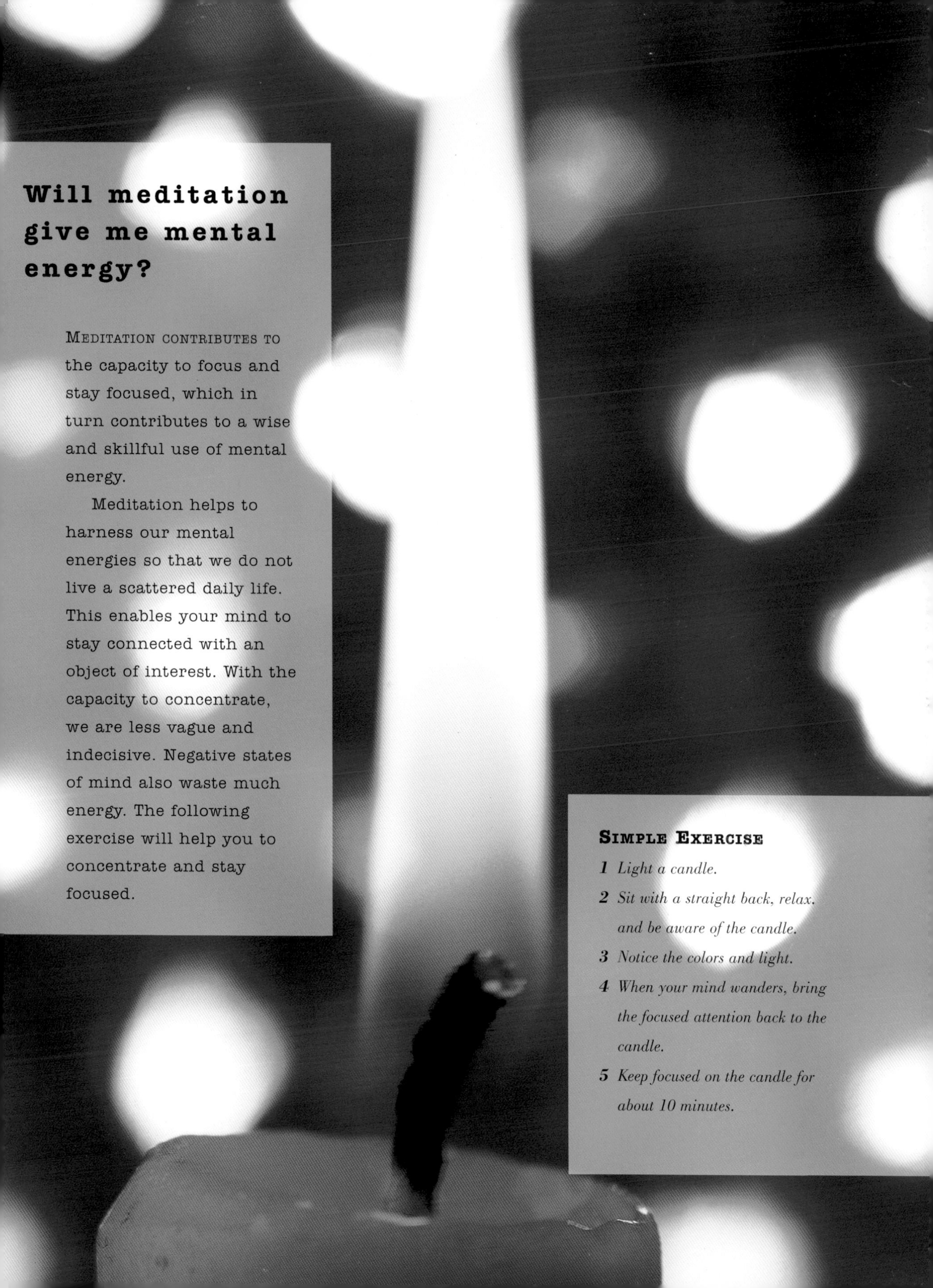

Will meditation give me mental energy?

MEDITATION CONTRIBUTES TO the capacity to focus and stay focused, which in turn contributes to a wise and skillful use of mental energy.

Meditation helps to harness our mental energies so that we do not live a scattered daily life. This enables your mind to stay connected with an object of interest. With the capacity to concentrate, we are less vague and indecisive. Negative states of mind also waste much energy. The following exercise will help you to concentrate and stay focused.

SIMPLE EXERCISE

1 *Light a candle.*

2 *Sit with a straight back, relax, and be aware of the candle.*

3 *Notice the colors and light.*

4 *When your mind wanders, bring the focused attention back to the candle.*

5 *Keep focused on the candle for about 10 minutes.*

In the moment of creativity there is a flow of energy, expression of imagination, vision, and single-pointed attention. In that moment, creativity expresses health in the psyche.

Will meditation increase my creativity?

WE KNOW THAT certain artists have led very tortured lives, and they may have drawn upon that experience for their art. But great art also comes from peace of mind. Eastern traditions have recognized that in the depths of meditation there is a huge reservoir of unexpressed creativity that can flow out of us. The following exercise will help you to release any feelings of restlessness, and channel your energy into one continuous flow.

Awaken feelings of joy
To move, jump, and dance can channel your energy into one harmonious flow.

SIMPLE EXERCISE

1 If you are feeling scattered, get up and dance with arms outstretched for about 10 minutes.

2 Move the body slowly in different directions.

3 Feel the flow of energy as you move many parts of your body.

4 Keep the flow going for the full period.

Will meditation help relationships?

Hurt, disappointment, and anger often arise in relationships. We expect ourselves to forgive and forget when we are unable to do either.

MEDITATION IS NOT an escape from confronting such situations, but is a way to deal with them more effectively. If we are still burning up or hurting inside, we have not yet got over the situation. In such circumstances, it is not unusual for the other person involved to get satisfaction from knowing that they can still press our buttons. It is certainly no easy task to rise above the situation. In some cases instead of being forgiving or letting go, we may need to develop equanimity, namely that capacity to stay steadfast in the face of a situation. We need to be clear about whether or not the situation can change. For example, the other person has ended the relationship and you know that this is

Russian wedding rings
Life is an interconnected experience. Try to remain steady instead of becoming entangled.

a final decision, then the primary meditation is one of acceptance. Clear, unconditional acceptance of change. All our willpower, neediness, and demand will not change that situation. Meditation on equanimity and acceptance can go a long way to finding peace of mind. We can sit quiet and still for 3 minutes through being mindful of breathing. Then we repeat inwardly the following words or similar expressions, slowly and mindfully in our mind, allowing the phrases to settle deep into the psyche.

FOR EQUANIMITY

May I be steady in this period of change.
May I be present in this period of difficulties.
May I stay centered in the heat of the moment.
May I be free from clinging to the past.
May I be free from clinging to the future.

FOR ACCEPTANCE

May I accept the facts.
May I not fight against the facts.
May I appreciate that the closing of one door opens another.
May I not indulge in resentment, blame, and hurt.
May I be at peace with the situation.

IT IS QUITE IMPORTANT that we should have an understanding of energy. We may be familiar with the scientific formula that $E = mc^2$, but this has little or no meaning for our daily life. Our concern is for the quality of energy as well as the quantity. Meditation can recharge our mental batteries, make us feel more alert, and provide us with calm resolve. This gives us the capacity to handle different situations rather than get caught up in reactivity.

We can use the energy gained from meditation for selfish ends: status, boosting income, and driving ourselves even harder during the day. It might impress our colleagues, but there will be a price. We will become blind to the needs of loved ones, to the wonder of life, and to a depth of knowing ourselves.

What does it mean to energize the body and mind? Conventional thinking is that we only get energized through the impact of something on our senses: sight, hearing, smell, taste, and touch. It can be anything from watching a goal being scored in a sporting match to the sudden outburst of a creative idea, or even an angry thought. In any case, there is a sudden shift from low to high energy in a single moment.

Meditation works differently from conventional thinking—it conserves energy wasted in countless thoughts, stress, and resistance. We use up energy when we cling to the past events or hopes for the future or neglect our physical and emotional life. A joyful energy is released through awareness, meditation, and a sense of the spiritual. Through meditation we touch deep levels of being, not only solving underlying problems in our inner life, but also gaining access to a bright, focused presence in the moment. Meditation on the body, feelings, nature, reflections, and associated daily practices will both conserve and create energy.

You will find that one of the wisest applications of this energy is through love, compassion, and action born of experiencing the profound awareness of the interconnection of all aspects of life.

Will meditation give me alert presence?

Getting Started

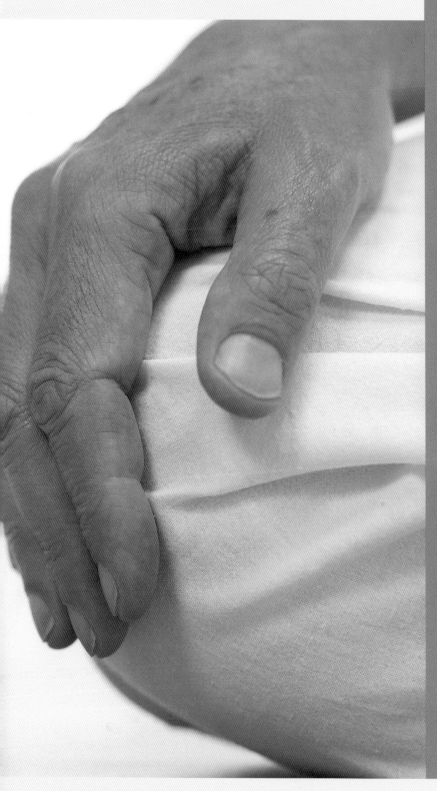

The Mudra of Touching the Earth is performed by resting your hand on top of your knee while kneeling. It reminds us of the significance of invoking the Earth as a witness to living with wisdom.

Most people can recall their first exposure to meditation. It may be through following instructions in such a book as this. It may be through attending classes, workshops, a meditation retreat, or spending time in a monastery. My initial reaction to meditation was not unusual and it may be encouraging to people who experience similar feelings.

MY FIRST MEDITATION teacher, Ajahn Dhammadaro of Thailand, gave me my initial instructions, and told me to practice them as often as possible during the day. He told me to sit still, cross-legged with a straight back, and moment to moment, raise my hand up and down in the air. My forearm was straight. I then moved my forearm from elbow to fingers up a few inches at a time until my hand almost reached my shoulder. Then I repeated the movement until my hand came down near to the thigh muscles of my leg.

He told to me to experience the warmth, and tingling arising in my fingers, the palm of my hand and my arm as I

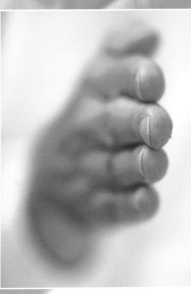

Each moment is mindful
Slow mindful hand movements help to train the mind to pay attention to the moment.

slowly moved my hand up and down through the air. It was extremely hard to sustain this for one hour. It was not what I imagined meditation to be and I could not see the purpose of it. At times, I felt doubts arise in my mind. My body began to hurt. After some days, a thought struck me clearly. I realized how important my right hand is. I began to appreciate that the meditation was contributing to my inner awareness. Suddenly my meditation practice was transformed from a rather mechanical and repetitive activity to an appreciation of the relationship between my mind and body. My hand was a statement of my inner life.

MINDFULNESS OF BREATHING

THIS MEDITATION, the core
meditation in this book,
contributes significantly to
clarity and peace of mind.
It is beneficial in a wide
variety of situations,
especially when it is
important to stay calm and
focused. Mindfulness of
breathing is used widely in
sports such as tennis, golf,
and swimming to keep
present and steady in each
moment. As a meditation
practice, mindfulness of
breathing makes us
accessible to depths of
awareness and clear seeing
into the way things are.
This practice helps free us
from reactivity which
arises in fear, anger, and
confusion.

Breathe deeply in and out
*Become aware of all the different
physical sensations as you breathe
deeply in and out.*

PRACTICE

1 In the sitting posture be mindful of the total breath experience.

*2 Experience your body expanding with the inhalation and
contracting with the exhalation.*

*3 Notice when the air brushes past your nostrils, both on its inward
and outward journeys.*

*4 Experience the incoming air coming up through your nose, going
past your throat, down into your lungs. As you breathe in, notice
the expansion of your body. As you breathe out, experience the
settling down of your body.*

5 Be aware of the moment(s) of stillness before the next in-breath.

*6 Train and develop yourself to be clear and present in the comings
and goings of the breath.*

Relax on the Out-breath

If we feel restless, we breathe long and deep, relaxing with the out-breath. We then repeat the process, by taking in very long, slow, and deep breaths, and breathing out similarly. If we feel a little light-headed after a few long in-and-out breaths, then we just return to steadiness and stillness. Willpower in meditation can generate pressure and tension, sometimes producing headaches. Instead we should apply a gentle effort.

We become aware of the breath as it comes and goes. All events, experiences, thoughts, and our states of mind share the same characteristic of coming and going. If we are experiencing some pain in the body while sitting, deliberately relax on the out-breath while relaxing any tension that may be building in the body from the pain.

We become aware of the kinds of sensations arising with the in-breath and out-breath: warmth, vibrations, pulsations, tingling, tension, whether comfortable or uncomfortable. Observe carefully the touch of the beginning of the breath on the body and the end of the breath.

If you feel very tired and sleepy in the sitting meditation, then use an alternative method of slowly raising the arm (elbow touching the ribs) up and down, slowly, so each movement has a beginning and an end to it. Pay attention moment to moment with eyes open or closed.

Air is life
Breath acts as a bridge between the mind and the body.

Use a Counting Method

The air element confirms our intimacy and interdependence with the surrounding world. This perception contributes to our liberation from self-centered existence. If necessary, it is worth using a counting method at the beginning of the breath meditation for the first few minutes. In the counting method, we count each out-breath from one to ten, and then return to one again. If we lose our way or the mind wanders and drifts, then we start again from the beginning. We should take care that we do not end up just counting and being out of touch with the breath.

Practice Your Breathing

We need practice to know the difference between relaxing contact with the breath, and trying to control the breath through placing pressure on it. The practice is developing simple mindfulness of breathing without using force of the mind over the breath. Initially, the breath may be rather erratic and unsettled. If

Breath training is practical
Mindfulness of breathing has its practical applications, such as playing musical instruments or participating in sports.

we are quietly patient, it will begin to settle down naturally. Using willpower over the breath tends to create tension. The fact of turning our attention to the breath will have some influence upon it. This influence will reduce as we develop greater harmony of body and mind.

It is important that we continue our practice even if we feel we are making slow progress. It is not unusual to experience these feelings. As we develop our meditation practice, we will begin to feel the benefits. Beware of others who treat meditation disdainfully. Always remember that they are not speaking from their own experiences, but just expressing their own unfounded opinions. It is your experience that counts. If meditation is contributing to your well-being, contentment, and clarity, then simply ignore the negativity voiced by others.

Postures

SITTING

IT DOES NOT matter whether we sit cross-legged, use a meditation bench, or sit on a chair without any back support (unless it is necessary). The position of our legs has no relevance. We don't have to be influenced by the countless images of cross-legged yogis in meditation. With the sitting posture it can be wonderful to have a special quiet place in our home for this meditation. It might just be a cushion, stool, or chair in a room free from clutter. We might face into the room or face the wall.

In the sitting posture:

- *Check the whole presence of the body from head through to toes*
- *Turn your attention to the details of the posture*
- *Rest your head easily on your shoulders*
- *Tuck chin in slightly*
- *Roll the hips forward and lift your diaphragm and chest area*
- *Be receptive to the present moment*
- *Practice not clinging to any thoughts, words, and ideas in your mind*
- *Experience calm presence one moment at a time.*

Every moment you are mindful of the present is a moment of meditation. You do not have to try to force the meditation to achieve some idealized state. Depth will come naturally. You have made your contribution through the willingness to sit in an upright posture, eyes open or closed, and be receptive. If it is easier to be present and relaxed with your eyes open, then cultivate eyes-open meditation as opposed to closed.

Be conscious of breathing. ***Practice for 20 minutes.***

Warmth
Use a shawl or blanket for extra warmth and comfort if helpful.

PRACTICAL SUPPORT FOR FORMAL MEDITATION

Three beneficial supports for meditation in the sitting posture are:

*1 **Zafu**. A zafu is a firm, round cushion filled with kapok (a cotton-like substance that grows on trees), around 10 to 12 inches (25 to 30 cm) deep and 12 to 14 inches (30 to 35 cm) across. If your legs go to sleep, experiment with the cross-legged position or use an extra cushion. Place a folded blanket on the floor to give support to your ankles and legs.*

*2 **Meditation bench**. The bench often has a padded surface. You adopt a kneeling posture with your legs under the angled bench. It keeps your back straight with less pressure on your legs.*

*3 **Chair**. Use an upright chair, possibly with a firm cushion, not an armchair. Only use the backrest of the chair if you have a history of back ache.*

WALKING

All postures matter equally in meditation. Formal walking meditation is a form of contemplative expression. This means that we walk unusually slowly. We might walk slowly up and down the length of our room. We begin by checking our posture from head through to the toes. We place one hand on our abdomen, and the other hand on top of it. We walk respectfully to the presence of life lifting each foot up very slowly, moving it through the air so that the heel of one foot barely goes in front of the toes of the other. We keep the head and trunk of the body very still. The eyes are kept ahead looking at the ground two yards ahead. We only need a short distance to walk up and down. Experience the subtle shifts and changes in the energy and weight through each foot as it touches the ground or floor. The act of walking matters more than the preoccupation with destination or where we are coming from. In meditation, what is matters more than what was or what might be. *Practice for 20 minutes.*

STANDING

There are plenty of opportunities for standing meditation. We may be waiting to meet somebody at a predestined place. When we lose touch with the moment, it is so easy for unpleasant mental states, such as boredom, impatience, blame, and doubts to arise. We forget that wherever we go, there we are. In standing meditation, we check our posture from head to toes, both our feet are fairly close together, our body perfectly upright. Unlike soldiers, we are not under pressure to stand to attention. Our practice is to experience a relaxed presence in the whole body, especially in our feet's contact with the floor or ground.

Standing meditation can also transform our whole relationship to the place where we are standing. We check through our body to see if there are any areas of tension in our shoulders, lower back, calf muscles, etc. We direct our attention into those areas to relax them. Initially, the standing period may only last for a few minutes without discomfort. We can then switch to a little walking meditation before returning to our standing meditation.

It is not unusual for people in the Orient to practice Tai Chi meditation in public places before going to work. I hope the day will come when people elsewhere practice their chosen meditation whether sitting, walking, standing, reclining, eating, or movement openly without feeling self-conscious. *Practice for 20 minutes.*

RECLINING

In reclining meditation, we lie flat on our back with heels together, or we bend the knees so the heels are drawn close to the buttocks. We can lie on a carpet, a firm mattress, or a lawn (preferably in the shade). We then place our head on a small, firm pillow or use two or three books. Our arms are straight down the side of our body with our palms facing upward or downward. When our body is quite still, we feel its presence and contact with the mattress or ground.

We keep very still. Our eyes can be open or closed. In this posture, we let our whole body relax, including the mind. It might be that we drift into sleep in these moments. This is fine. On waking, keep the posture even for just a minute or two, before moving. If we keep falling asleep, we can raise one of our hands

Reclining posture
In the reclining posture, the body is kept very straight and perfectly still. All of the body is consciously relaxed onto the floor or mattress.

with the fingers pointing toward the ceiling or sky. This will help to maintain our alertness. Reclining meditation can be quite useful when there is pain in the body or we find it difficult to sit upright, but we may need to use extra effort to prevent ourselves from falling asleep.
Practice for 20 minutes.

EATING MEDITATION

There are two initial considerations for eating meditation:

1 Diet

Eat a nutritious diet with food that is easily digested, such as fruit, vegetables, grains, and protein. The amount of food you need will depend on your metabolism. Insecurity, anxiety, and force of habit affect the amount we eat. Contentment of mind contributes to balanced eating practices.

2 Mindfulness

Mindfully bring the food to your mouth, mindfully chew the food, and mindfully swallow it. We experience from moment to moment the different tastes of our food and drink. By the time the food is swallowed, it needs to be almost liquid. It is helpful to eat slowly without rushing our meal to aid our digestion as well as our peace of mind. We can also take a single item of food such as a currant or a piece of banana and make it an eating meditation. We become totally aware of the whole process of our teeth chewing on food.

Healthy eating
We must consider what we eat, the amount we eat, and the speed at which we eat. All these factors contribute to our physical health.

3 Mindfulness

Mindfully, we bring food to our mouth, mindfully chew the food and mindfully swallow it. We experience from moment to moment the different tastes of our food and drink. By the time the food is swallowed, it needs to be almost liquid. It is helpful to eat slowly without rushing our meal to aid our digestion as well as our peace of mind. We can also take a single item of food, such as a currant or a piece of banana, and make it an eating meditation. We become totally aware of the whole process of our teeth chewing on food. We can appreciate eating without simultaneously reading a book or newspaper. Just as we appreciate contact with others, we can also appreciate mindful contact with ourselves. At the end of the eating meditation, it is worthwhile to reflect on appreciation and gratitude, such as:

Nutrition
A nutritious daily diet contributes
significantly to a long and healthy life.

- *May the farmers and their families who produced this food live in peace and harmony. May their crops and animals be supported*
- *May they not be stricken with floods, droughts, and hardship*
- *May their relationship with the land nurture them and their communities*
- *May all those who transport the food from the farms travel safely*
- *May they and their families be well and happy*
- *May all those who work in markets, stores and supermarkets be well and happy*
- *May their day be free from pressure and strife*
- *May all live in peace.*

Movement meditation

MOVEMENT MEDITATION can take various forms, such as cycling, dance, jogging, yoga, or martial arts. There is something energizing and creative about mindful movement whether we do it alone, with a partner, or with a group. These days many people love the experience of going to an outdoor concert where there is the opportunity to stand and move the body.

In movement meditation, we move gently and purposefully, experiencing every part of our body. For music lovers, there is classical, rock, and new age music to accompany every mood. Movement meditation can help relax tensions that build up during the day, or can serve as a preparation for sitting meditation.

Jogging is one way to keep in touch with bodily energy, contact with breathing, and nature. I have recognized the importance of the mind in long-distance running. While running a marathon, my mind wandered, owing to bodily tiredness. As a result, I would start to slow down. Mind influences body and body influences mind. Running and fast walking can transform energy flows. When we energize the body through exercise, there is natural access to altered states of consciousness, alertness, rhythm, and harmony. This feeling of connection with life and the earth is a wonderful result of genuine presence.

We can develop our practice to move and explore in each meditation of this chapter. They can become regular features of our day whenever we are sitting, standing, walking, or reclining. ***Practice for 20 minutes daily.***

Cycling
Avoid rushing to reach your destination and enjoy the rhythm of cycling.

Times for meditation

MEDITATION ENCOURAGES us not only to live one day at a time but also to live mindfully throughout the duration of the day. When we are willing to give extra attention to the fullness of each moment, we can know a deep sense of conscious living and being connected with what is around us.

Routine
Getting up, going to bed and times of appointment can easily affect our inner life.

MORNING

To meditate at the beginning of the day takes effort and discipline. We may have to put cold water on our face and stretch our body for two or three minutes to feel ready for the first meditation of the day. It may require a change of attitude as well as routine. We stop rushing around to get ourselves, and perhaps others, out of the house. We start the day mindfully, unhurriedly. We make each act count. We bring presence to what we do. We include in that the willingness to sit and meditate. If the first tasks of the day take longer, then we rise earlier giving ourselves the opportunity to act mindfully.

Some meditators start the day at sunrise. They set the alarm to coincide with the first break of daylight. Perhaps you will want to take a walk to welcome in the new day, or place a chair by the window to look out as the new light comes in. If there is quite some time between the dawn and the need to get ready to go to work, we can go back to bed. The body can adapt to two sequences of sleep, or we can lie there quietly, being mindful of our breathing.

In the morning, some people experience only waves of tiredness, especially in sitting meditation. If this is the case, it is important to keep your eyes open, rarely blink, and focus on something immediately in front of you, such as a candle, a religious object, or even a patch of color on the carpet.

Refresh yourself
Splashing cold water on your face in the morning stimulates the cells, refreshes the skin, and contributes to an overall feeling of alertness.

EVENING

The evening time is invaluable for meditation. We have come home from work or study, finished our meal, done the dishes, and so forth. Often when it is all finished we just want to slump in an armchair. If we are to bring in a period of evening meditation, it might not be wise to leave it as the last task since we might not have any energy left. We may have to be prepared to leave the dishes, or start the evening meal later. We can devote the same amount of time as with the morning meditation, about 20 minutes. Some regular meditators sit longer—anything up to an hour, twice a day. Quality comes before quantity. (In Chapter 5: 20 Meditations for Daily Life, I have given a number of specific meditations once you feel well established with the breathing meditation.)

Priorities
What comes first—washing the dishes or meditating to clear your mind? Meditation should be your priority.

BEDTIME

Some people have difficulty getting to sleep. It seems the channel between waking and sleep gets interrupted through body sensations, sounds coming through our ears, or various thoughts. Generally, it is better to go to sleep after our food has been digested. However, for people who have great trouble in sleeping, it might be useful to drink some warm milk, or eat a banana, or both before sleep. The thought "I can't sleep" can stimulate the mind into reactivity, so we maximize the degree of relaxation by letting our whole body settle into the mattress. We keep our body perfectly still and relaxed to maximize the state of restfulness. With practice, the channel to sleep should get easier.

Meditating at night
Meditating in the middle of the night contributes to profound inner peace.

MIDDLE OF THE NIGHT MEDITATION

We wake up in the night and there is silence. We are aware of countless millions of people in our hemisphere who are fast asleep at this time. Instead of going back to sleep, we can appreciate the grandeur of this silence. When we develop our appreciation of silence, we can experience a deep sense of rest.

We can use this time for sitting meditation or horizontal meditation. It can be useful to sit upright on your bed, steady in a cross-legged position with a spare blanket around to keep you warm. Or you can go to your meditation corner. If you feel tired the following day, it is important to take some extra rest or sleep. A short nap in a chair can be remarkably restful.

Working with Difficulties, Knowing Contentment

The Mudra
of Receptivity
is performed
by sitting
cross-legged
on the floor
or in a chair
with our
palms facing
upward. We
remain open
to whatever
unfolds.

To know ourselves is to live at peace with ourselves. When we do not know ourselves very well, we keep experiencing reactivity in the mind. Our mind creates a pattern of certain difficulties that can arise frequently.

BUT FORTUNATELY we are not stuck with these patterns; we can change this situation. When we work on these patterns, we take the power out of them. This brings not only contentment and clarity to our lives but also access to depths of experience that are unavailable if we are living in a reactive way. Various difficulties can arise in meditation as well as in daily life. Resolving any of the following 12 common problematic areas brings inner peace:

- *stress*
- *compulsive thoughts*
- *worry and fear*
- *anger*
- *putting off tasks*
- *force of wanting*
- *force of habit*
- *boredom*
- *restlessness in the body*
- *impatience*
- *doubt*
- *lack of self-acceptance.*

Each one of these difficulties is unpleasant, unwanted, and unnecessary. They produce a troublesome state of mind affecting the quality of our life as well as that of others. They can get a grip over us that is hard to shake off. Eventually the anguish fades away only to reappear again later in similar or different circumstances.

Physical signs
Our private inner life becomes public through our body. If we are happy and content, it will show through our eyes and mouth.

Stress

WHEN THE STRESS and frustration in our lives reaches a certain level, we begin to feel nothing is going right for us. We make mistakes and cannot concentrate. We become intolerant and demand even more from ourselves. Never underestimate the impact of stress. It weakens our immune system, tires cellular life, and produces negative thoughts. As we age, the ability of our mind and body to tolerate stress decreases rapidly.

Stress combines the dual forces of the desire to get things done, and the fear of not getting things done. To combat stress, we may have to consider making changes to our outer life. Do we find ourselves trying to do too much, too quickly, too soon, and too often? It would be self-deception to imagine that we could continue like this and still have an energized mind and feel relaxed throughout our whole being.

"Do I want to change?"

"What am I prepared to change?" It may be vital to ask yourself one or both of these questions until you feel the urgency to bring about change. Investigating these questions should generate greater awareness about the causes of your stress, and encourage you to take practical steps to reduce it. Sometimes that means learning to let go of things that dominate our life.

You may need to spend a silent day away from everybody and everything to put problems aside and turn your attention to the way that you are living. It will give you the opportunity to reassess your priorities. You might reflect on practical changes and make a short list of things to do immediately. Be aware that resolve fades quickly! Then, you may want to draw up another list, focusing on what you are neglecting as a result of busyness and stress. Regular meditation practice is a fine resource for dealing with stress.

Negative thoughts
Time goes slowly when we are waiting and impatient, causing stress and negative thoughts.

Compulsive Thoughts

A COMMON compulsive thought is the one that we have so much to do that we can never get enough done. These thoughts can persecute us. Even when we do get things done, we think that we could have done better. Sometimes our thoughts keep going over and over the same issue. It is imperative that we break this loop. One method that can help is done using the standing posture. Stand very, very still and give your mind an opportunity to relax.

CASE STUDY

I knew a young man who found that within the first minute of his meditation, the same lines of a song kept going over and over in his mind. He asked me what to do. I asked him how often he listened to music. He laughed and said he was a musician. I told him to cultivate silence. I advised him to listen to music only when he could give it his full attention. I then suggested that he write down the words of the repeating song. Were the words revealing something to him? I reminded him that this same groove in the mind can produce painful and obsessive thoughts. In his meditation he needed to keep his eyes open and maximize his connection with silence in the here and now. Compulsive thoughts often indicate reactivity. They can signify a desire for self-gratification, negativity, doubt, or fear. It can help to write down these thoughts, and ask ourselves:

- *What is the essential demand in these compulsive thoughts?*
- *Am I committed to letting go of obsessive thoughts through changing the object of my attention?*
- *Is there another way to look at this situation?*
- *Do the circumstances of my daily life have to change?*

Music
Appreciation of silence heightens our appreciation of music, and vice versa.

Worry and Fear

PEOPLE EXPERIENCE an enormous amount of pressure in their lives. Meditation will be more helpful if we acknowledge these pressures.

Worry is often a result of pressure. Anxiety springs from unclear perceptions and feelings. It becomes a background noise in our daily life. To dissolve worry, we must practice to breathe mindfully. This will help to overcome anxious thinking. We also need to develop the ability to look at a situation in a different light.

The trouble with fear is that it keeps us from doing what is appropriate and necessary. We may wish to bring about meaningful change in our lives, but fear will not allow us to take these steps. Unpleasant feelings and thoughts can arise, and in turn, produce fear. Through the power of meditation, we develop the capacity to act, and stop these thought patterns when they begin.

We might want to make one huge leap for change, from fear to fearlessness, but one should be patient. Permanent change should take place gradually.

Small steps
Sometimes it is necessary to remember the significance of taking one small step toward liberation.

CASE STUDY

A woman spent a long time in a mental hospital several years ago. Patients on the ground floor were close to release while those on the fifth floor were far from it. She was on the fifth floor. She wanted to leave the hospital, but she had a fear of the outside world. A nurse had an idea to help her make her journey back into everyday life by asking her to take just one step towards the door on the fifth floor. The nurse then marked the spot with a line of chalk. The next day the patient took another short step forward, starting with her heel on that chalk line. The nurse then drew another line where the foot rested. Despite the strength of her fears, the patient slowly, step by step, made her way to freedom. Day by day, the patient moved forward, down through the floors and weeks later, she walked out of the hospital. We may have to approach some of our fears in the same light. Being too ambitious about overcoming a fear can be a way of preserving it.

Anger

ANGER IS A BIG ISSUE for many people, whether it shows in lingering resentment, explosive outbursts, or frequent negative mind states. It is one of those unsatisfactory conditions of mind that makes life difficult for everybody. If we recognize this, it should increase our determination to sustain a practice of freeing the mind from this condition.

Three major factors that cause anger are:

- *We are blocked from getting what we want*
- *We feel hurt. We cannot handle this feeling, so we blame or attack others*
- *We cannot cope with the outcome of events.*

From the spiritual standpoint, there is too much anger, resentment, and hatred in the world already, so we work to transform reactivity to action, love, or wise criticism. We may need to practice letting go of a situation so that our anger does not burn us up. Open communication about our feelings and thoughts with a clear and responsible perception contributes to dissolving the pain of anger.

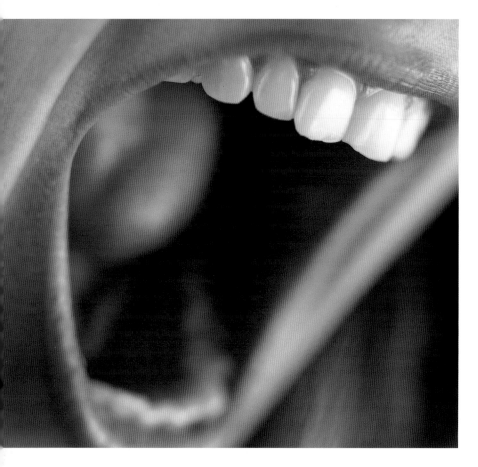

Anger is destructive
Anger can be destructive to your emotional life.

Putting off tasks

WE OFTEN USE the future as an escape from action by making numerous plans about what we will do later. It is a way of avoiding engagement and contact with today. The future becomes a big, black hole into which we put our fears, hope, fantasies, and daydreams. Meditating on breathing here and now gives the mind an opportunity for calmness, concentration, and presence. In India, a sign in a store window said: "Cash today. Credit tomorrow." If we give care and attention to today, we will lose this tendency to procrastinate, which otherwise can run throughout our life. It can set us up for feelings of failure and disappointment. If we look after today, then tomorrow will look after itself. We have to remind ourselves that if we take two steps forward and one step back, then we are still making progress. This is a practice.

- What specific task are you going to embark on?

- Do you have to let go of other involvements to fulfill a task?

- Having a balanced life means the capacity to say yes and no.

- Here is a way we can practice giving attention to something here and now:

  1 *Take one task today that is neglected.*
  2 *Apply yourself to it.*
  3 *Finish it.*
  4 *Stop and appreciate its completion.*

Pressure
Pressure in our daily lives can build up like a pile of laundry. It is important to find the time to do what is necessary, but also to find the time to relax.

The Force of Wanting

SOMETIMES WE EXPERIENCE a tremendous desire for something. This wanting can become a real pressure in our minds. We feel that we will not have any peace of mind unless we get what we want. This can lead to unhappiness and disappointment. By combining reflection with meditation, we can come to know our priorities and discover ways to achieve realistic goals wisely.

Play and have fun
When we are overworked it is often at the expense of play and fun. Children and adults playing together contribute to each other's happiness.

CASE STUDY

John worked in a freight yard for many years. The heavy work caused strain on his lower back. His doctor prescribed rest and medication. Neither seemed to relieve the pain. He then began to have more and more difficulty coping with the pain. He became irritable. His children avoided him, and his wife found him difficult to please.

John decided to explore two alternatives. He went to visit an osteopath for treatment, and he began to engage in meditation to explore, under guidance, that area of pain in the lower back. Within a few weeks, the lower back pain that had troubled him for more than two years faded away, and the force of the wanting mind went with it. His wife and children were greatly relieved when they saw the difference.

Regular meditation practice gives us the power to accept what must be accepted and the energy to start changing what can be changed.

We must ask ourselves:

- *What do we want?*
- *How dependent are we upon succeeding for peace of mind?*
- *What is a balanced attitude to our efforts?*

The Force of Habit

THE FORCE OF UNHEALTHY habits makes us wonder how much freedom of choice we have. The first step to changing such habits comes through maximizing our awareness of them as much as possible. We must be very clear in ourselves that we have to work on any unhealthy habit daily. Smoking is an example of an addictive habit. There is a significant concern over smoking apart from health issues. It suppresses the emotional life. We are feeling worried or agitated so we reach for a pack of cigarettes and light up to inhale the smoke to cloud out our unsettledness. In the course of time, smoking tends to have a deadening effect on all of our senses as well as harming cellular life.

Bad habits
No harmful habit is easy to give up. It is the daily determination to give up a bad habit that counts.

CASE STUDY

Mary smoked two packs of cigarettes a day. She knew it was stupid. After smoking for more than 30 years, her voice had developed that rough rasp. She hated herself for her addiction and became negative and irritable when she could not get her hands on a cigarette. She noticed the desire for a cigarette. She could feel the sensations of the wanting in her body, in her feelings, in her thoughts, and her every movement as she reached for the pack. Even when she pulled a cigarette out, and picked up her lighter, it was still there. The moment she lit the cigarette and took her first puff, the yearning and wanting faded away. One day she realized that cigarettes didn't give her peace of mind, but only acted as a relief from the force and the pressure of this habitual wanting.

I suggested to her that she should increase her practice of mindfulness of breathing for as many minutes in the day as possible. I encouraged her to make a commitment not to smoke a cigarette for an hour after a meditation, and to replace a cigarette with a full glass of fresh water every time she had a desire to smoke. Her motivation was strong. Some weeks later she wrote and told me she had finally broken the habit.

Ask yourself:
- *What will strengthen my resolution to break a habit?*
- *What will weaken it?*
- *What can I do today to show that I am serious about breaking it?*

Boredom

ANOTHER FEATURE of a difficult inner life is boredom. Disappointment, unresolved negativity, fixed routines, and habitual ways of seeing others and ourselves can result in boredom. The use of alcohol, drugs, tobacco, and caffeine can bring temporary stimulation. But the high that takes place can bring about a corresponding low, leading to feelings of boredom. If our priority is our inner health, then spiritual practices, depths of meditation, making love, sport, and entertainment can enable a natural flow of energy. Sleep then becomes a vehicle for the renewal of energy. Paying attention to our thoughts can bring insight into our tendencies toward highs and lows.

Dissatisfaction
Be aware of the masks we wear to cover various forms of dissatisfaction.

CASE STUDY

A retired woman travelled overseas for a wonderful visit with her son and grandchildren. When she returned home to her small apartment, the place seemed very cold and empty. Owing to jet lag, she had much trouble in getting to sleep. She felt despair and loneliness. She began to miss her son and grandchildren very much. But then she realized that these emotions were simply the combination of thoughts and unpleasant feelings. Immediately some of them began to lose their hold over her. She made a hot drink, turned the heating on, put on some music, and started to organize her return home. She began to feel glad to be in the quietness of her own surroundings once again. Situations like this make us grateful for our meditations on watching the arising and passing of thoughts so that we do not slide downhill into despair.

PRACTICE

- *Start each day as a new beginning in your life*
- *Start each day as though it were the last day of your life*
- *Take one risk for each day*

Restlessness

MUCH OF OUR SENSE of worth tends to be tied up with our perceptions of our body. It is important that we accept the aging process unconditionally as it takes place from moment to moment. Moment-to-moment meditations on change will help to prevent us from living in resistance or denial. The body belongs to a whole movement and process of life, rather than to the whims of the self. A calm and comfortable relationship with our body shows itself in the capacity to relax into the process of life, no matter at what stage of life's journey we are traveling. Moment-to-moment meditations on change will help us with this relaxation.

What is our relationship to our color, gender, height, size, and weight? We can build up distorted and judgmental perceptions about ourselves. Do we need to practice letting go of some of these interpretations? It is no easy task to use the mirror with discretion without getting caught up in various self-images. Trying to appear beautiful, youthful, and energetic can later produce resistance to loss of beauty, aging and lowering of energy levels. The capacity to meditate on the body helps to cut through many of the projections we have around bodily appearance.

PRACTICE

- *Regard the body as organic life in the web of existence*
- *Acknowledge the interdependence of mind and body*
- *Say as a mantra—birth, aging, pain and death—to be honest with the cycle of life.*

Embrace nature
The body is an expression of organic life.

Impatience

FRUSTRATION AND IMPATIENCE can easily turn to anger if we are not careful. By focusing on the causes of these feelings, rather than the effects, we can work toward building the patience and understanding necessary for a positive and happy life.

CASE STUDY

Angela was a single mother with two small sons who she found to be a handful. Her frustration grew and changed from impatience to anger. She then hated herself for being so hard on her children. Angela realized that other factors were influencing her attitude, such as a shortage of money, lack of free time, and an attachment to tidiness. She knew she had to focus all her mental energies on the practice of patience. She began to take deep breaths instead of raising her voice. She stopped making threats, and expressed more appreciation for her boys. It was not long before Angela began to feel better in herself, and her sons, naturally, noticed.

Doubt

DOUBT CAN BE a crippling state of mind. We get a great idea to do something. The idea is within our capacity providing we follow the initiative through. Then the mind starts producing streams of doubts that undermine the whole idea. Our doubts then gain more power than the original vision. We need to develop enough concentration to get back to the original idea, to keep faith with it, if we know it is for the welfare of ourselves and others. Doubt is worthwhile when it helps us to discover when our action might result in suffering, conflict, or anguish.

Lack of Self-Acceptance

LACK OF SELF-ACCEPTANCE is one of the most pervasive personal problems in our society affecting countless people to varying degrees in all age ranges and social categories. Feelings of lack of self-acceptance or lack of self-worth can haunt our daily life. When caught up in these feelings, we never feel good enough. This can produce unfavorable comparisons with others. The mind deceives itself when it believes that self-worth comes through increasing our workload or gaining the approval of others who matter to us.

Self-worth comes through appreciation and acknowledgment of our existence, not dependency on others. We experience our worth as a person through knowing ourselves, being grounded, creative, and connected with daily life. We learn to stop believing in the judgmental voice from within that erodes confidence and makes us feel inept. That harsh judge within us all comes from the feeling of pressure. That voice is an echo of something old. We learn to ignore it. We cultivate awareness, communication, and action in daily life.

Be understanding
Children are untidy. This is normal.
When we forget this simple truth,
everything starts to get on top of us.

Influence of Thoughts

WE HAVE PROBABLY all had the experience of having what we consider the best thoughts in the world, but find they do not have the power to make any real difference to the quality of our life. One function of meditation is to bridge that gap. Some thoughts can arise along the lines of "I must start;" "I must stop;" "I must change." These are all well-intentioned thoughts springing from the acknowledgment of unsatisfactory situations. Unfortunately these thoughts have no power to change circumstances, no matter how well intentioned. Yet the mind does have the capacity to influence real change. This is one of the many great powers of meditation. It can bring about inner change, sometimes remarkably quickly.

Meditation empowers beneficial thoughts and provides the capacity for us to let go of futile ones. A focused attention should replace vague intentions and circular thinking. Going over and over matters of past, present, and future can stop us from getting any kind of peace whatsoever. Fears and fantasies can dominate our thoughts and being preoccupied with self-image and time blocks our access to a clear relationship with daily life.

Meditation on Watching Thoughts

SOME PEOPLE have the idea that the purpose of meditation is to cut off all thinking. This is a misunderstanding. Meditation practice enables us to work wisely with streams of thought. It is beneficial to end indulgence in daydreams, and flights of fancy. Take time to observe the thoughts that accompany your speech and actions. In our meditation, we practice to:

- *Be aware of both negative and caring thoughts*
- *Be aware of the impact of a substantial set of thoughts*
- *Remember that a thought is just a thought*
- *Practice witnessing the coming and going of thoughts*
- *Notice the space between the thoughts.*

If you follow the detailed instructions given in this book, it will help you to clear your mind from the excesses of thinking. There is a certain sequence that takes place with streams of thinking, and part of meditation practice includes learning to watch and recognize those streams. It includes:

- *Initial contact with an impression or thought*
- *Feelings arising on such a contact*
- *Thoughts arising dependent on the feelings*
- *Intentions and desires arising from the feelings*
- *Fixation about the intentions and desires.*

After an argument, we can continue to carry the residue of impression, like resentment, toward that person, causing an unhealthy stream of thoughts and feelings.

Learning not to carry the residue of impression contributes significantly to our peace of mind.

Meditation on Feelings

There are two common types of people:

- *Those who feel controlled by their feelings and emotions. They get fired up quickly, making life distressing for themselves and others*
- *Those who become removed from their feelings. This may show as lack of warmth, or being distant from others. Or it may show as being very intellectual.*

The following meditation acts as a support for both types of people. We use the following practice to learn to stay in touch with our feelings without becoming either overwhelmed or removed from them.

- *What is the feeling here and now? Is it pleasant or unpleasant or something in between?*
- *Can you stay steady with this or are you looking for something more?*
- *Is there the wish to be with feelings, intensifying them, or to escape from them?*
- *Acknowledge feelings of happiness, contentment, and friendship. Feel the quality of such experiences*
- *Be watchful of rigid views and opinions that come from strong feelings*
- *Be clear when feelings are superficial and when they are deep.*

Clinging to pleasant feelings leads to desire and the pursuit of self-interest. Clinging to unpleasant feelings leads to withdrawal, aggression, or other forms of reactivity. Clinging to indifferent feelings leads to ignorance and blindness. A wise connection to our feelings is the antidote to clinging.

Hot tempers
Aggression is common amongst people who are not in control of their emotions.

Meditation on States of Mind

IT IS IMPORTANT that we
acknowledge clearly a passing state of
mind as just that; passing. If we don't, it is rather
like looking at the world through a pair of dark-colored
sunglasses and believing that the world is dark. We also tend
to form strong views about ourselves through associating "I" and
"my" with our current states of mind. The practice of seeing a state of
mind as only that gives a sense of space around it. It will then have less
of a grip over us so that we can recognize its arising and passing. Some
states of mind which are painful and obsessive may well require the support
and skills of another who can see our state of mind for what it is and guide
us through it.

There are also the states of mind born from the joy of depth of meditation,
ecstatic experiences, and rushes of energy in moments of contact or insight.
Such experiences are to be appreciated and fully acknowledged, but as with
painful states of mind, they are not worth clinging to. Trying to repeat
such experiences often leads to disappointment or
frustration later.

PRACTICE

- *Remind yourself that this is the
  present state of mind without
  clinging to it or rejecting it*
- *In formal meditation, practice
  to be aware of the state of mind.
  It might be focused or
  unfocused, calm or agitated,
  clear or cloudy*
- *Appreciate the quality of the
  clear mind*
- *See the mind as an expression of
  an unfolding process rather
  than a personal problem*
- *Acknowledge creative expression
  and freedom of the mind.*

States of mind
*Some states of mind
can only be achieved
through the depths
of meditation.*

Energy and Healing in Meditation

The Mudra of Meditation is performed by one hand resting on top of the other in a posture of calmness and stillness that will contribute to steadfastness of mind.

The Relationship of Mind and Body

Through experiments, scientists and psychologists have observed the links between the brain, the body, and the immune system. Messages constantly travel between the brain and the body affecting the health and well-being of each other. Meditation acts as a practical approach to directly exploring the relationship of our feelings, thoughts, and states of mind to the body, and vice-versa.

The mind and body influence each other in many ways. Scientific journals report that the lines of communication between the brain and the body get infected through addiction to alcohol, drugs, smoking, and other forms of substance abuse. Unhealthy states of mind, such as anger, worry, and loneliness, impact on the organs and cells of our body. This impact easily affects our sleep, diet, exercise, and our relationship to our body.

Meditation on mind and body includes observing the mutual influence between the two and the impact of our emotions. Emotions act like waves and can be pleasant or painful. For example, when somebody says something that embarrasses us, our cheeks suddenly become red. When we laugh, we feel warmth running through the body.

Scientists believe that in the future they will be able to predict latent genetic tendencies to some kinds of illnesses. If the time comes, it might increase our level of worry about the future rather than increase our clarity and ability to make wise decisions.

Meditation is an important stabilizing influence in the acquisition of knowledge about our circumstances.

Mind and body
The mind and body affect the well-being of each other. Regular meditation is an excellent stabilizing influence.

Personal Relationships

FIXED ROUTINES can have a gradually destructive impact on relationships. We often forget that the quality of time matters far more than the quantity of time. It is quite possible for two people to be together in the same home but never actually meet each other in real terms. A relationship is about love, awareness, and communication, not just habitual, close proximity. Sometimes hurtful things are said that can linger in the psyche. If someone has said or done something that we have difficulty coping with, there can be a loss of trust. In these instances, our meditation must be focused on the here and now, rather than lingering on the past event. If we linger in the past, there will be no hope for renewal.

This applies in situations between parents and children, close family members, and many other relationships. We must practice being present and connected with what is happening here and now. The past is for learning, for understanding, and for reflection, not as a weapon either against others or ourselves.

We may find we are unable to cope with personal problems arising from a relationship. Our mind becomes so unsettled that we cannot meditate during this period. At these times, it is important to resolve to return to regular meditation practice. The past, recent or distant, can exert a relentless pressure upon us. If so, we should turn to counseling, therapy, or the wise perceptions of a reliable and honest friend. Working with the past requires openness. For example, if we have experienced loss and disappointment in a relationship, after we have talked it through, we renew contact with regular meditation so that we keep in touch with the unfoldment of life. Awareness, meditation practice, equanimity, and acceptance will reduce the time gap between disappointment and appreciation of new challenges in our life.

Body Meditation

Once reasonably proficient in mindfulness of breathing, we can turn to body meditation. We can practice this meditation while sitting, walking, standing, or reclining (see Chapter 2). We are extremely conscious of the presence of our body without thinking about our body or analysing it.

1 PRACTICE

Moment to moment, scan your attention slowly from the top of your head down through your body to your feet then go back up through your body.

2 Turn your attention to the top of your head. Experience the sensations that are present all over your head and face and then your neck, especially the throat. Move the attention down the front of your body from the top of your chest to your genitals. Then from the top of your back to your buttocks. Then through each arm to the tips of the fingers. Then from the top of each leg to the toes.

3 During the journey down and up through your body, experience the feelings of warmth, vibrations, and tensions. There may be times when you feel nothing at all, but keep your attention moving from one moment to the next. The power of attention contributes to dissolving pain and tension. This reduces restlessness in our body, takes reactivity out of our minds, and grounds us deeply.

4 The length of time you choose for this meditation may vary. For some people, 10 to 20 minutes may be enough. You may wish to go more slowly and take as much as a half hour to go from the top of your head through to your toes. When practised regularly, you will notice the areas of the body where there is tension, pressure, aches, and pains. In a relaxed way, we can direct mindfulness into these areas, resulting in changes in vibrations and sensations. With this meditation, we learn to be at ease with the body, including pain, sickness, and aging.

Working with Pain

PAIN IN THE BODY may arise through an injury from the past or present, or from sickness, due to either hereditary or genetic factors. Carelessness can also cause pain, carelessness due to something we did to ourselves, like putting excessive strain on the body, or from somthing someone did. In order to feel more at ease in the pain, in our meditation we witness the outer edges, as well as the epicenter of the pain. We observe the way the sensations change, their impermanence. We explore the whole region of that pain. We may notice any reaction that is taking place within ourselves at that time. It might be that another part of the body begins to tense up. We find our mind resisting pain, or the desire to escape from it. We do not make this practice an endurance test. If there is too much pain, we change our posture for a few minutes and then perhaps come back to that posture again.

With practice, we can expand our pain horizons while acknowledging when appropriate to move, or to continue to work with pain in a certain posture. If in doubt, take the kindly view towards the body rather than use willpower.

When I go to the dentist, I decline to have an injection for fillings. (I might give a different response if it were root canal work!) I remember to breathe in through the nose, relaxing on the out-breath. I check the rest of

Pain
It is an enormous challenge to keep steady in the face of pain.

my body, especially the stomach and diaphragm area. I notice when there is any physical contraction in my body due to pain. Then I relax on each out-breath.

All of this is a simple training in moment-to-moment experience in the basic composition of organic life. As our meditation deepens, we become less reactive to bodily life while remaining respectful to it. We understand its benefits and limitations. We take care of it from one day to the next. We understand the changes as our body passes through the various stages of life. Wisdom is feeling at ease with bodily life, taking appropriate steps to deal with its condition. This wisdom is available through the regularity of meditation on the body.

In the old tradition of the East, the body was referred to as elements: earth, air, fire, and water. Or, to put it another way, the elements of hardness, movement, temperature, and cohesion. As we refine our body meditations, we can experience:

Earth
Direct attention to the skeleton

Air
Direct attention to the breath

Fire
Direct attention to the
warmth of the body

Water
Direct attention to blood,
sweat, tears, and saliva

Visualization Meditation

For this meditation you must use your imagination. You must be able to create a picture or symbol in the mind that can touch deep places in the heart, releasing healing energy. Visualization practices contribute to gaining access to devotion, joy, inner absorption, and healing of heart, mind, and body.

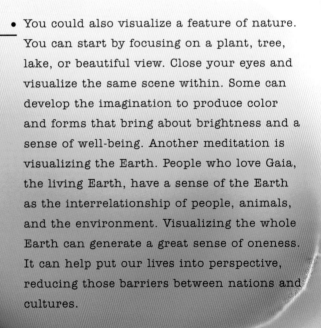

- We might visualize a symbol, such as the Star of David, the cross in Christianity, the yin-yang of Taoism, or the Wheel of Dharma in Buddhism. These symbols have been used in meditation for centuries to remind us of the place of religious or spiritual experience. A Buddhist abbot once meditated on the cross, the most famous symbol of Christianity. During his meditation, he realized that the cross could also symbolize the cutting of the "I", the ending of the ego. He then found a new depth to the message of love and liberation that Jesus gave.

- You could also visualize a feature of nature. You can start by focusing on a plant, tree, lake, or beautiful view. Close your eyes and visualize the same scene within. Some can develop the imagination to produce color and forms that bring about brightness and a sense of well-being. Another meditation is visualizing the Earth. People who love Gaia, the living Earth, have a sense of the Earth as the interrelationship of people, animals, and the environment. Visualizing the whole Earth can generate a great sense of oneness. It can help put our lives into perspective, reducing those barriers between nations and cultures.

Mantra Meditation

There are two kinds of mantra meditation. Each one can contribute to a deep sense of inner peace and contentment.

- One mantra includes a devotional element. We might repeat the name of our Supreme Being, for example. The mantra might be Hallelujah, Glory be to God, Praise to Allah, Hare Krishna, Buddha, or Jesus of the Heart. Such mantras used daily move us beyond self-preoccupation.

  The other mantra repeats a word to bring about calmness and stability. For example, the mantra might be "Be Here and Now," "One Step at a Time," "Love," "Be mindful," or "A friend to all." You might say the mantra 108 times (a number that represents infinity in some traditions of the East).

Sexual Healing and Physical Abuse

In order to recover from the traumatic effects of sexual or physical abuse, it is important for a full acknowledgement and recognition of the hurt caused by the event to take place within you. Meditation is one way forward in the healing process.

CASE STUDY

I remember once at a meditation retreat, a woman in her twenties asked to speak to me. She wept as she told me of how her uncle had sexually abused her as a child. She felt very angry towards him. In her meditation, she realized the way it had affected her relationship with men, and made her afraid of sexual experience.

I spoke to her of ways to move toward healing herself. She needed to continue the process of open communication about experiences and perceptions of the situation past and present for as long as it was felt necessary. She also needed to speak about it with someone she trusted. We agreed for her to develop a healing meditation toward her womb and entire area of sexuality by directing warmth, love, energy, and acceptance to this sensitive place. For this she would sit in a relaxed and comfortable posture.

PRACTICE

1 Feel the presence of the whole body without making any pressures or demands upon it.

2 Turn the attention to the area of the womb.

3 Approach the sensitive place from the outer edges.

4 Moment to moment, keep the attention at the area of sensitivity.

Recite these words (or similar ones):

May this area be healed.

May this area be free from the impact of the past.

May happiness and well-being be felt in this area.

May any suffering associated with the womb fade away.

May contentment and peace fill this region.

May my heart be open and receptive to the warmth and love of others.

May I be free from reaction to the abuser.

May I generate warmth and love for others.

May this healing process come to completion.

The young woman practiced this healing meditation daily. Gradually, she felt less hurt, less negative, and less afraid. It was a tribute to her willingness to address a very sensitive region of her life. At times, she found that she began to cry in her meditation or get very angry. So she would stop the meditation for a time but never abandoned it. She wrote later to tell me that she had found the strength in herself to write to her uncle to make it clear to him what she had suffered. She told him she wanted to meet and talk with him to try to understand how he could do such a thing. She said her uncle refused to see her. The young woman told me that she no longer felt hurt or angry with her uncle. She said she knew intuitively that her uncle could not face his history. "His response was one more thing I had to accept," she said.

8 Turn attention to the very center of the pain, hurt, or discomfort. Direct light and warmth to the whole region again and again.

7 Recognize the way that the past has prevented living a full life.

6 Acknowledge the effect of it.

5 Acknowledge the hurt that has taken place there. Be mindful of the history of pain.

There may be times when we are suddenly exposed to a life-threatening situation. The adrenaline flows. Scientists tell us that the brain secretes a hormone at the time of danger, stimulating not only the body, but consciousness as well. This acts as a potent resource to bring awareness to the forefront to face the circumstance. Life, of course, is constantly full of the unexpected.

A Life Threatening Illness

CASE STUDY

A young man in distress came to a retreat. His physician had just informed him that he was HIV positive. It had completely thrown his ordered life into total confusion. He was afraid to think about the future.

He felt distress about telling his parents and friends.

He dreaded coming into the meditation hall to meditate; he felt so much self-doubt and confusion. In one of the interviews he said, "I wish I was religious. I wish I believed in God. Surely it would be so much easier."

I replied, "For you, your breath is God. For you, contact with your breath is contact with God. It is the one resource that you have in the moment to stabilize your mind, steady your body, and dissolve all those feelings and thoughts that oppress you from within."

Later, I taught him a heart meditation. He had to open the lines of communication between himself and the virus. If he was in conflict with it, then he would experience pressure and fear. This would weaken his immune system.

The young man and his virus had to learn to coexist

together. I told him he had to develop a friendship with the virus. If he could do this, then he would not feel so threatened. He began to engage in loving kindness meditations, cultivating a warm feeling that he deliberately and consciously directed toward the virus. At one point he told me he gave his virus a personal name. By using a name instead of calling it HIV, he felt less threatened. The young man left the retreat much happier and with growing confidence.

Fear and anxiety
Use meditation to help dissolve the fear and anxiety you feel as a result of a life threatening illness.

20 DAILY
meditations

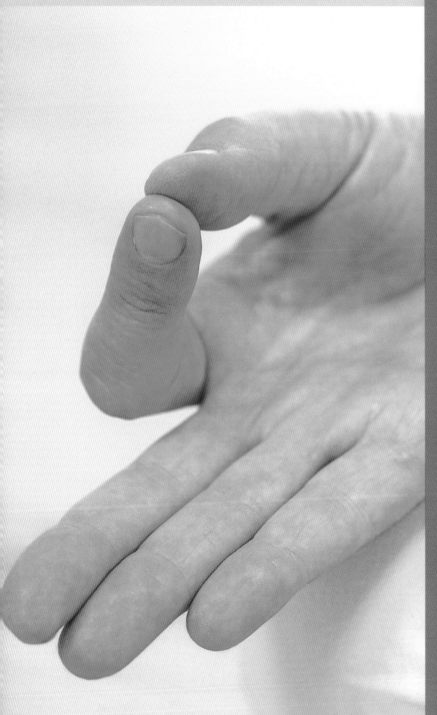

The Mudra of Inter-Connection is performed by the thumb and forefinger touching, symbolizing that everything relates and connects with everything else; the unity of all things.

Four Periods of the Day Meditation

Each of these periods of the
day matters equally. It is easy to get out
of balance in one area at the expense of another.
We so easily say, "Oh, I'm hopeless at the beginning of
the day," or "I have no energy left by the time evening
comes." We get used to identifying ourselves in this way, mostly
through not examining our relationship to each of the four periods.
Through practice, it is quite possible to develop or conserve energy so
that we experience each day as genuinely full, balanced, and complete in
itself. Finding this balance will reduce the separation between periods of
high and low energy. Eating breakfast with your partner and going to a
business meeting get the same quality of attention. Levels of energy affect
our state of mind. We can make unwise decisions with long-term costs in
a moment of high energy. If our energy is low, we can be more vulnerable
than we know. A person only has to say a harsh word to us and we can
feel hurt and reactive.
In a low energy period we can easily become less mindful and act
carelessly; we can make mistakes and unwise decisions. If we
develop a practice of connection with each of the four
periods of the day, we will love and appreciate the
challenge of each day. Life will not seem
so trapped in routine either.

1 *Wake-up to breakfast*

2 *Breakfast to lunch*

3 *Lunch to dinner*

4 *Dinner to sleep*

DRINKING TEA MEDITATION

In the Zen tradition, there is an exquisite tea ceremony. Something ordinary can become extraordinary through the power of mindful attention to every little gesture. Each of the senses can be highlighted one at a time. You can engage in the tea ceremony with others or alone. Every witnessed feature of the event is a moment of meditation.

1 Pour enough water into the kettle to make a pot of tea. Turn on the stove and observe the heat rising from the kettle. Sit quietly and listen to the sound of the water heating. Pour some hot water into the teapot to warm it. Then add spoonfuls of tea and more hot water. Wait 3 or 4 minutes; then stir the water in the teapot, put the lid on, and pour the tea mindfully into the cup. Smell the aroma of the tea arising.

2 Lift your cup of tea and mindfully begin to take a first sip. It is the silence and respectful mindfulness of drinking tea that makes it a meditation. After drinking the tea, continue in this silence until after washing the teapot. Acknowledge the beginning, middle, and end of the process. Mindfulness of drinking tea contributes to enlightenment.

LIGHT MEDITATION

This meditation contributes to dispelling moodiness, cloudiness, and darkness of mind. It is a meditation to increase your awareness and appreciation of light.

- Sit in a posture with your back straight.

- Keep your eyes open and be receptive to experiencing light.

- Allow the light in through your eyes and into your being.

- Stay with your eyes open, blinking only when necessary, while keeping the body still.

- Close your eyes and visualize light within yourself.

NOWHERE TO GO MEDITATION

It is not unusual to be standing in a line for a bus, train, or flight, or sitting in a traffic jam. We often say how tiring and stressful it is traveling to and from work. We forget that it might also be our attitude that drains our energy. If we stop clinging to the view that we have somewhere to go, and deliberately become aware that there is nowhere to go, we might feel different about being in the line. Wherever we go, there we are. Sky above. Earth below. This meditation makes us extraordinarily aware of the living present. There is the opportunity to feel the presence of our mind and body and surrounding environment. This meditation concentrates our mind, attends to cellular life, and releases more energy. Instead of feeling exhausted on the way to an appointment, we feel renewed.

Recite these words: There is nowhere to go. This is it. Then allow the words to fade away so that you begin to feel and experience the truth of the statement.

MEDITATION ON NATURE

Exposure to gardens, forests, meadows, mountains, rolling hills, the ocean, and the sky relaxes our whole being. Such experiences nourish our relationship with the miracle of the vast web of existence. We feel the colors, the sounds of nature, and the temperature upon our being without indulging in thoughts and fantasies. We commit ourselves to regular contact with the range of expressions of nature through the fullness of our attention. There is the opportunity to feel extraordinary oneness with all life. Practice of full attention increases and deepens our acknowledgment of what it means to be in this world.

HERE AND NOW MEDITATION

We provide a great service to ourselves when we remember to be here and now. At this time we should reduce our thoughts about the past and future. We learn to experience the present moment. We remind ourselves that every moment is a new moment, worthy of interest and attention. Instead of being bound up in time, days, pressure, and punctuality; consciousness awakens to the newness of the moment. Our experience of the here and now is confirmed through awareness of seeing, hearing, smelling, tasting, touching, and seeing clearly the state of mind or thoughts as they reveal themselves in the present moment.

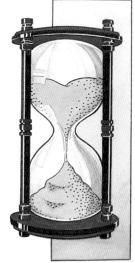

NOTING MEDITATION

This is especially suitable for people whose minds wander a lot in meditation. It is at times important to note specifically the state of mind or the general drift of the thoughts. We can use a single concept to state clearly in our mind what is happening. For example, if we are thinking a lot  about the past, we say, "memory, memory" to ourselves or if planning ahead we say "future, future" or "planning, planning." The practice of noting helps us to keep in touch with what is happening in the present moment. If we apply noting to the present moment, we might note "sitting, sitting" or "being here and now." This helps to give clarity to what is happening rather than continuing to indulge in thoughts. We can apply the same method to states of mind. We name the state of mind for example, boredom or restlessness in our meditation firmly and clearly, and then return to the original meditation object such as breath or body. Noting meditation enables us to remain sharp and clear and return quickly to the initial object of meditation.

CONCENTRATION MEDITATION

The capacity to concentrate, even for short periods, gives empowerment to the mind. For example, you might see a runner on the racetrack staring straight ahead, keeping the body very still, very meditative before the race. They might close their eyes, keeping their mind totally concentrated on the task at hand. It brings their whole being and their aim closer together. This is a way of combining the body energies for the task at hand and the mind's subtle energies so they work in cooperation. We need to be mindful that we do not overstep ourselves. Unwise ambition leads to disappointment and anger. Problems tend to arise through making too great demands upon ourselves and others. Clarity and self-knowledge are required to know how far it is wise to extend ourselves. As a practice, we can concentrate on something we see while keeping our eyes still.

DANCE MEDITATION

We have much to celebrate through being alive, though we often forget this. Dance is a deep communication of celebration. It is a way of expressing the wonder, joy, and mystery of life. In the free-flowing movement of dance, our ego can drop away. There is no consideration for the dancer. The dance is all. The ego loses itself in the dance so that the flow and the rhythm of the dance itself take over. We dance to God, we dance to life, and we dance to express oneness with the dance of life. There is no special form to this dance, nor any special place for its expression. We are not dancing to impress others or ourselves. It is a statement of joy, love, and ecstatic harmony with all things. So dance!

SURRENDER MEDITATION

Cultivating posture and state of mind together can contribute to awareness, devotion, and surrender. For example, we might sit in a chair, or cross-legged with a hand on each knee, palms facing the ceiling or sky. We close our eyes and bring a smile to our being. We start to feel a smile coming from our face through relaxing the facial muscles, and then gradually letting that smile extend itself right through our body from head to toes.

When the pleasant feeling has pervaded all the cells, head to toes, we allow ourselves to surrender to life. We offer up our existence to the nature of things. At first, this might seem a rather shallow and superficial meditative exercise, so we cultivate and develop it until it deepens. As it does so, we begin to sense the truth of the situation, namely that our life does not belong to ourselves; it belongs to the nature of things. In walking meditation with the palm of one hand resting on the abdomen, the other hand on top of the back of that hand, we walk slowly. We surrender to each step, to each moment. The meditations on surrender are an important contribution to our awakening.

FASTING MEDITATION

We have heard about yogis and saints who engage in long fasts as a feature of their meditation. There are other ways to fast that may be more beneficial for our health. We might fast once a week, drinking only water for part of the day say for six hours or maybe even 12. For one week, we might fast by abstaining from a particular food, such as cookies or chocolate. Such ways of fasting act as an inner discipline and benefit for both body and mind. It is unwise to go on a complete fast, drinking only water for more than 48 hours, without supervision. Some people believe that fasting and meditation must go together so they fast for several days. After the fast, they can easily swing to the other extreme and want to eat enormous quantities. It is best to keep in mind the middle way, namely moderation in all things. Eating a nutritious, easily digestible, simple diet in moderation contributes to balance and contentment.

MEDITATION ON FLOWERS

By common consent, flowers are one of the most beautiful gifts of nature. We love to see them in the garden, in our home; we love to see wildflowers in nature. Some people have a special love for flowers and are familiar with their names, characteristics, and seasons. For the love of flowers to flow deep, they must become a meditation. Just as flowers stay still, only swaying gently in the breeze, so we too must stay still, or sit still to be able to feel a deep sense of harmony with flowers.

To meditate on a flower, let your eyes lovingly look at every detail, every expression, every color, and its totality. A single flower can awaken us to its breathtaking beauty. If we develop regular meditation on a flower, we will attune to the other flowers of life, from the beginning to the end of the day. There is also the fragrance that emerges from a flower. As we engage all of our senses in the experience, our meditations on the flower enable us to experience the mystical fragrance of existence.

STANDING IN THE FOREST MEDITATION

When we take a walk in a forest, we often forget that our walking in the forest is in contrast to the trees. Trees stand still with their roots running deep into the ground. Forest meditation is to be as the tree. Stand very still. A friend of mine once walked to some nearby woods to be as a tree. She stood very still. After a few minutes, she saw two deer pass close by. Then she saw a fox, a squirrel, a badger, and wood pigeons. She said afterwards: "I saw so much more by standing still than I would have done by walking." It also gave her a greater and deeper sense of being close to the trees.

COLOR MEDITATION

There has been quite a lot of research into the way that colors affect us and reflect our mood at a given time. Green can communicate closeness with nature; blue— infinite expansion, such as the sky or ocean; and red—heat and vibrancy. We can give time to focusing on one color, then give time to another. This heightens our appreciation and receptivity to the diversity of color that comes to our eyes. We need to be aware of the colors of our clothes. Is it wise to wear black if we feel in a dark mood? We can also limit ourselves to a particular shade of color. If we have a fixation about a particular color, it means our perceptions are limited. As a result, we can end up running madly from one store to another to find it. Expanding our appreciation of the range of colors also expands our mind.

HAPPINESS MEDITATION

In this meditation, we become settled, relaxed, and steady with an upright posture. We then turn our attention to an experience that makes us happy. It might be contact with a loved one, a particular place, a feature from nature, or our spiritual truth. We allow the happy feeling to come out of our heart. Gradually we allow the image or thought to fade away leaving the feeling of happiness. Practice cultivates this feeling until it pervades our cells. Happiness is within. There is a no path to happiness, happiness is the path. At the end of the meditation, we conclude with "May all beings know happiness."

EQUANIMITY MEDITATION

Equanimity is the capacity to stay steady and poised between two strong forces of the mind. One is the force of attraction. The other is the force of aversion. We feel the pull toward an impulsive purchase that we can ill afford. We breathe in and out keeping the body upright until the force loses its grip over us. We notice the desire to move in our meditation due to an itch. We relax into the itch using the power of mind to dissolve it.

The thought arises to do something else instead of meditate and we let the thought go. In these ways, we are cultivating equanimity towards attraction and aversion. Such a practice contributes to developing the mind to face much greater dramas of life with equanimity.

MEDITATION ON IMPERMANENCE

This is one of the most important meditations in the Buddhist tradition. One Buddhist abbot said: "We are all brothers and sisters in birth, aging, pain, and death. Impermanence meditation is a meditation on endings—the end of the breath, the end of a stream of thoughts, the end of a task. It is knowing clearly and deeply that whatever arises also passes. Meditation on our impermanence will make clear to us the limitations of control and choices that we have. We see impermanence as a fact of life affecting everyone and everything. Awareness of our impermanence keeps us in touch with change, comings and goings, rising and falling, birth and death. We experience impermanence through moment-to-moment attention. The practice on impermanence takes the terror out of loss and death.

These are some of the benefits of the meditation on impermanence:

- *It enables us to be clear about the finiteness of our existence*
- *It helps to keep in check the unquestioning desires of the mind*
- *We are less likely to take anyone or anything for granted*
- *It can contribute to enabling us to deal with aging and the processes of life.*

It is an honest meditation to help us keep in touch with change, with the birth and death of events. In this meditation we do not adopt a gloomy attitude to impermanence. There are many times when we are grateful for change. We may refuse to accept change. This makes for another kind of pressure. Staying in touch with moment-to-moment, day-to-day changes keeps the mind open and receptive.

MEDITATION ON DEATH

We can look at departed relations and acknowledge their birth and death, their joys and sorrows. We reflect: "Just as all others have come into and passed out of this world, so I have come into this world and will pass out of it."

It is not a despairing kind of meditation. Far from it. It is a way to acknowledge the processes of life, so that there is no denial in our existence. Such meditations can help to dissolve greed and demands on others. We cannot take any accumulations with us. If in this meditation we begin to feel unhappiness or despair, it indicates that a negative state of mind has entered the perception. We also need to be aware of birth and death, arising and passing, of this state of mind too.

A beneficial time for death meditation is when we go to sleep. In deep sleep, all thoughts of past, present, and future, including everything about our existence, enter into oblivion. When we are worrying about the future and the end of our life, in a way, we are not really living. Those who do not live, fear death, not those who truly live. Death complements life, as night complements day.

INFINITY MEDITATION

1 Sit in an upright posture, indoors or outdoors.

2 Be aware of space. Be present to the space between objects, between you and what you see.

3 Listen as well. Sounds come and go in the ears. Be aware of the space that embraces all of the sounds.

4 Be aware of the distance and depth of space and the way it contains the many different things of life.

5 Turn your attention inward and be aware of the space between thoughts.

6 Be aware of the sense of space deep in the body and in all of your cells.

7 Open out the awareness to embrace space inwardly and outwardly simultaneously. In this meditation, we need to remain mindful of not becoming spaced out.

8 Continue in this meditation providing you are quite stabilized and grounded.

TOTAL PRESENCE MEDITATION

This meditation is the experience of total presence without taking up any particular object whatsoever, such as the breath. In this meditation all things are treated equally. We acknowledge the vast web of existence embracing all things.

In total presence, there is the embrace of unity and diversity. This meditation helps diffuse the whole sense of ownership, of having and possessing. It is a real key to understanding the nature of things without our mind constructing views and opinions, whether philosophical, scientific, or religious. In this meditation there is neither promotion or demotion of self. This meditation reveals the vast web of existence.

COSMIC MEDITATION

1 On a warm and pleasant night, find a quiet, open, dry space to lie down outside, perhaps on a mat, keeping very still.

2 Have your feet together, arms beside each other, with palms facing upward.

3 Spend a few minutes looking at the night sky. Be aware of the depth of the universe and the expanse of it.

4 Feel your place in relation to everything else.

5 Know how everything is interrelated, near and far.

6 Feel the extraordinariness of it all.

7 Let appreciation and gratitude for the mystery flow.

8 If fear arises (it sometimes happens through feeling vulnerable or insignificant), then reflect on the number of other human beings who have to pass through these difficult experiences. Allow it to be a further confirmation of your connection with everything and everyone.

Communication, Change, and Clarity

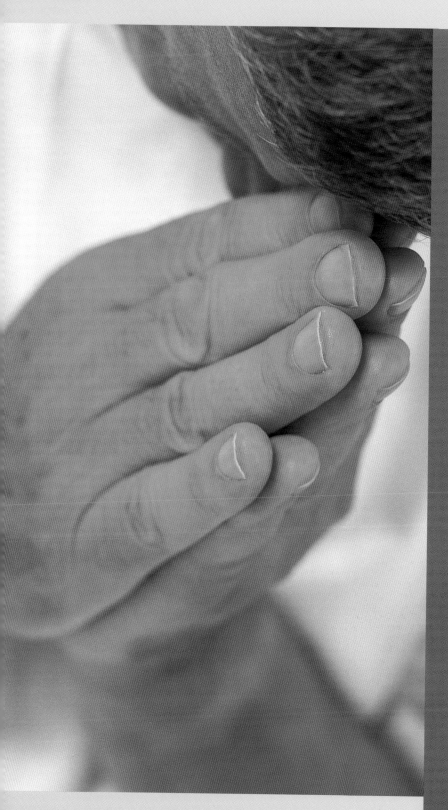

The Mudra of
Prayer pays
tribute to
the vast
presence of
life that is
so much
greater than
our personal
existence.

Mobile phones
Some forms of communication offer convenience, but not necessarily quality.

Aspects of Communication

To FIND CONTENTMENT in our daily life means that we should attend to all aspects of it. We need to practice and develop the skills to approach each day with clarity, concentration, and dedication. Some believe that the motor for action is tension, stress, and anxiety, otherwise we would procrastinate. That may be the experience of some people. It would seem a human tragedy to abide in stress and anxiety to force ourselves to do things. We can achieve significant benefits through making small changes in the way we experience the day. Our attitude and relationship to concepts matter as much as our responsibilities.

Meditation on "work"

THE WORD "WORK" can bring immediate resistance: "Oh, I've got so much work to do;" "I hate this job;" "My life is going from one task to another." Others think, "I'm unemployed. I really want to work. I've got nothing to do all day." Such people have inner pressure around the very concept of "work." There is often emotional and psychological baggage around the word. We can drop the concept of "work" and view the totality of our each day differently.

PRACTICE

- *Begin the day with formal meditation*
- *Give extra attention to letting go of thought about tasks for the day*
- *Drop the language of "work" from your speech*
- *Regard the day as a moment-to-moment unfolding activity rather than going from one task to another.*

Such a practice helps to break down the investing and compounding of "work" in the mind. We easily get caught up in reactivity around starting work, ending work, finding work, losing work, too much work, not enough work. These perceptions fragment the day. We practice in order to experience the fullness of each day rather than to have a divisive view of it.

Coffee breaks
A heart to heart conversation over a cup of coffee can make the world of difference in a busy day.

Mindful Communication

THE WAY WE COMMUNICATE affects the quality of our lives, and the lives of others. We can bring clarity and contentment to a situation or we can bring confusion and resentment. We may think that yelling abuse at other people may get them to wake up. Our bullying tactics may only succeed temporarily. As time goes by, such a strategy becomes less and less effective. The audience for our reactivity either withdraws, becomes submissive or becomes resentful. When we become determined to get our position across to another, we lose sight of important considerations such as:

1 Is this the right person?

2 Is this the right time?

3 Is this the right place?

4 Is this the right subject?

If we are out of tune with any of these, it may be difficult to reach a mutual understanding in any important conversation. For example, we might seek somebody's advice, but he or she lacks clarity and a balanced view of a situation. This means we have not chosen the right person. Or in another case, we have some issues with a loved one. We want to resolve the problem, but it is unwise to start an intimate discussion late at night when the other person is tired and just wants to go to bed. Wrong time. No matter how fired up we might be, we might aggravate even more conflict and misunderstanding.

There are six aspects of communication worth paying attention to. If we are mindful to cultivate and develop all of them, they become a daily meditation.

AWARENESS

Be aware of the detail and general experience of the event, related circumstances, and our behavior in it. We remember to speak as accurately as possible if we wish to be listened to. To inflame or deflate a situation is unfair for the listener. It is a practice to be able to relate what happened, or is happening, or what will happen, in a language which is as honest, clear, and precise as possible. We reflect what we receive.

FEELINGS

Are our feelings pleasant, painful, or somewhere in between? We might need to begin our communication with "I feel ..." Otherwise we might make claims that we are speaking an absolute or objective truth.

THOUGHTS

Various thoughts probably occur before an important communication. Our thoughts may have tried to predict what the other person(s) will say but communications often do not work out as planned. We need our minds to be as clear and steady as possible. We also need to be aware of the thoughts arising during communication which can block listening. If we cannot listen to another person, then there is little chance of another listening to us. Trying to impose our thoughts upon another often brings resistance or submissiveness, not understanding. Those who have a submissive attitude in times of difficulty may later resent the pressure from the other person.

INTENTIONS AND MOTIVATIONS

What do we want from the communication? Are we reasonable? Are our intentions colored with desires, projects, and fantasies? If so, we may not realize how out of touch two or more people can become with each other. It requires much self-honesty to be aware of our intentions. Are we showing wisdom and kindness, or looking to satisfy our ego, or hurt the feelings of another?

Confidences

At times we may need to be very mindful of what we say to one another. We need to be respectful to any intimation of confidentiality. Breaking of confidences brings confusion and guilt.

INVESTMENT IN RESULTS

If there is a lot of personal investment in getting our own way, there is little chance of reaching agreement. If determined to get a certain result, we can become increasingly out of touch with the process itself. Attachment to results easily produces fear and anger. Mindful communication is one of the areas requiring much attention. Meaningful communication takes place in a safe and supportive environment.

I AND MY

We need to be aware of the strength, frequency, and attitude arising in communications that involve "I" and "my." Does the other person(s) have equal opportunity to speak? It is not unusual for people to find it rather tedious to listen to someone who can do little else but talk about themselves or their opinions. Some people in small groups wait to be asked to speak rather than initiating communication. A primary consideration in communication is that we should treat others as we wish to be treated.

Mindful communication is a daily practice. Like formal meditation, it requires attention, interest, and a capacity to learn. Desire for attention, need for approval, and inconsiderate claims inhibit mutual understanding. If we neglect attention to these issues, we create suffering for ourselves and others. When we indulge in lies, gossip or back-biting, we unsettle the minds of ourselves and others.

We develop communication skills to overcome nervousness, impatience, and confusion that can make us sound unsure of ourselves. We may also need to make it clear to another if we find what they are saying is unacceptable or irrelevant. There is little point in listening to a litany of somebody's negativities. In an intense meeting, mindfulness of breathing becomes an additional resource to sustain calmness and clarity. It is helpful to practice it afterward, as well, rather than going over and over what was said.

Caught on tape
If we could record our daily conversations at random, would we be surprized to hear the things we say?

Listening Meditation

IMAGINE, WE ARE sitting at the airport waiting for our flight to be called. There is plenty of activity—flight announcements, people talking, and the buzz of different sounds. Our listening meditation attends to all three types of sound, namely, voices, machinery, and nature. We listen to the space between sounds. The sounds come to our ears. Vibrations touch the body. Some sounds enter our being and have a noticeable impact on our various distinguishable, life-stimulating feelings.

These feelings arise and fall. In an open, spacious, and receptive mode of listening, the sounds can pass right through us. It seems as though we are transparent. There is the throb of life all around. We are an empty form that is not disturbing such activity. There is no need for any special reason or motivation for the listening. The act of listening is reason enough. We are not listening for pleasure nor for obligation. There is simply the presence of the listening itself—an all-embracing awareness of moment-to-moment existence.

Headphones
Listening to music can be relaxing, but headphones can isolate us from the rest of the world.

Meditation and Sexual Intimacy

SEXUAL EXPERIENCES involve heart,
mind, body, speech, and action. In India,
Hindu and Buddhist religious authorities realized
many centuries ago the importance of the relationship of
sexuality to religious experience. The Karma Sutra, a sacred Hindu
text, offers various descriptions of postures that contribute to the
energy, subtlety, and intensity of sexual experiences. This is extremely
different from orthodox religion in both the East and West which has often made
a division between body and soul, so-called sins of the flesh and upliftment of the
soul. We need to embrace the field of sexuality as an expression of awareness and
meditative understanding. To bring meditative understanding to making love is to
cultivate deep inner qualities including respect and sensitivity. In a sexual relationship,
this means giving support, joy, and pleasure to another as much as to oneself.
Non-meditative sexual relationships tend to be charged with desire to reach a climax
as quickly as possible followed by exhaustion and sleep. This may be satisfying to one
and disappointing, if not hurtful, to the other. In meditative sexual relationships, the
participants learn to listen to each other and develop awareness and sensitivity of the
various movements. Language also expresses love and communication. Before
making love, two people need to get to know and trust each other.
It is important to know what each other appreciates in sexuality, where the
sensual areas are, and how creative imagination can be used through
posture, time, place, and interactivity. When we are willing to nourish
all of this in the light of a meditative awareness, then there is
much less likelihood of sexual experiences becoming
unreasonable demands upon each other.

Lovemaking

*To make love in creative and respectful ways
requires awareness, sensitivity and knowing
the joy one is giving to another. Genuine
lovemaking embraces deep consideration for
the needs of the other person.*

This meditation provides the opportunity for two people to connect with each other in silence.

Lovers' Meditation

- *You sit cross-legged or in a chair and face the person in front of you. Both of you are close together*
- *You may hold hands or have them resting on your knees or in your lap*
- *Let the warmth of your heart out through your body, out of your eyes and toward the eyes of your lover*
- *If it feels appropriate, you may sway your body from side to side*
- *From time to time, some words of love may pass from your lips to the ears of the other*
- *You experience each other's warmth and presence from head to toes.*

Sex and sensitivity, love and passion keep sexual energy alive for partners. Some yogis claim that meditation and spiritual practices require celibacy to conserve energy. This is a view born out of a celibate tradition, but that does not necessarily make it indisputable. We have to listen to our inner voice and experience about this. It is not unusual for sexual behavior to release energy, allow it to flow, and uplift consciousness—quite the opposite to what some yogis claim. We listen to ourselves to see what works in our lives.

Making a connection
It is important that two people take time to know each other, to experience mutual warmth and connection in the heart and in the eyes.

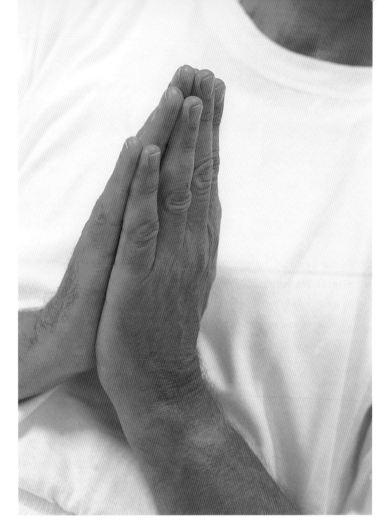

Prayer

Prayer can bring us closer to something greater than ourselves.

PRACTICE

- *Meditate on yourself as a small wave in the vast ocean of existence. As you go deeper in your meditation, become absorbed into the ocean of existence. All is water, nothing more.*

Meditation as Prayer

THERE ARE TWO KINDS of prayer. One has obvious expressions of self-interest. The second brings us closer to something greater than ourselves. In the first form of prayer, we ask for something; it is a request, a supplication. The small self, sometimes lovingly or in a needy way, calls upon something greater than itself for help or support. It is not unusual for human beings to call upon God in times of danger or loss. Even the hardened atheist may find themselves calling on God. Prayer can be abused through praying for self-gratification, a bigger car, more money, and a more influential job. But noble prayer invites surrender, intimacy, and absorption into the Supreme.

Signs of a Cult

THERE ARE COUNTLESS numbers of religious and spiritual organizations. Many show a wise, tolerant, and healthy approach to spiritual matters. However, we need to be aware of groups whose primary goals are conversion and empire-building, displaying intolerance to others. Such groups may reveal unresolved problems around leadership, power, and dogmatic beliefs. We need to be vigilant about some of the warning signals of such questionable organizations. These include:

- *Holding onto a central authority and narrow-minded claims to historical significance*
- *Strong identification with the leader or a book, and the adoption of dogmatic views*
- *Unresolved need of the leader to dominate followers and frequent use of "I" and "my" or "us and others"*
- *Closely knit family, obedience, and belief in superiority of viewpoint*
- *Dismissal or intolerance of others outside their circle, their beliefs, practices, and teachings*
- *Dependency instilling fear or rejection or guilt when experiencing genuine doubts.*

We can explore the range and depths of meditation, drawing from the experience and insights of others without having to become involved in questionable beliefs and organizations.

Cults
Spiritual materialism is a common feature of cults. Cults often financially exploit their members.

Diet and spirituality
Although we are not what we eat, our diet certainly has an impact on our spiritual lives.

Ways Toward Inner Change

CONSIDERATION TOWARD inner change includes:

AWAKENING
There can be experiences that suddenly transform our whole perception and priorities in a single moment or in a certain period in our life. From that moment, there is a turnaround in our consciousness. It leads to new values, new priorities, and the generating of love and liberation in life.

CHANGE OF LIFESTYLE
A growing number of people find affluence is not fulfilling. They realize that even more affluence will not bring fulfillment. This brings about a reflection on lifestyle. This may generate the intention to live with greater awareness, sustainability, and simplicity.

CONSCIOUS USE OF RITUAL
Probably the most noted ritual in the West is attending a church service on a Sunday. A danger with ritual is that instead of contributing to a sense of awakening and presence, it can have a numbing effect. Yet engagement in rituals can genuinely open up our consciousness. It might be that we resist religious ritual without ever taking the time to experience it.

CREATIVITY
It would be a pity to let a single day in our lives pass by without some genuine expressions of creativity. Our meditations will nourish this wonderful feature of life.

DIET
In India, a vegetarian diet has always been regarded as an indispensable feature of a deeply spiritual life. We can eat nutritious food without it being at the expense of other forms of sentient life. More and more people are becoming vegetarion for moral and health reasons.

GROUP WORK/COMMUNITY

Group work through retreats, workshops, meetings and conferences are short-term community experiences where we can learn as much from others as from ourselves.

MEDITATION

Meditation has two primary areas: calm and insight. The first contributes to well-being, health, energy, and healing. The second contributes to awareness, reflection, and insight into the nature of things.

MOVEMENT

Yoga, Tai Chi, jogging, massage, and dance all contribute towards inner change, relaxation, energizing mind and body, and that sense of oneness with the dance of life.

PILGRIMAGE

Pilgrimage highlights the journey itself with spiritual practices as a feature of that process. There are still many places of pilgrimage in the world.

PSYCHOTHERAPY

Psychotherapy can contribute to healing heart, mind, and body.

REFLECTION/SELF-INQUIRY

Wise thoughts emerge out of calmness and clarity, rather than a judgmental mind.

READING

Reading in a meditative way can contribute to a deeper understanding of ourselves.

RETREATS

These are a popular way to have a comprehensive experience of meditation.

SERVICE

This is a change in our inner life from getting to giving. Service springs from the conscious mind that cares.

SOLITUDE

Solitude contributes to our growth as a human being. Aloneness is voluntary and intentional, unlike loneliness which is unwelcome.

Reading
Reading can contribute to a deeper understanding of ourselves.

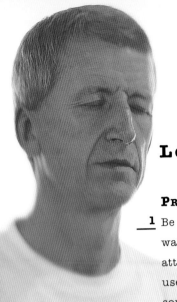

Loving Kindness

PRACTICE

1 Be relaxed and comfortable. Close your eyes and discover a warm, caring, loving heartfulness toward life. We do this by attending to the feeling of pleasant relaxation. If it is useful, we might turn our attention to somebody or something we love and appreciate. We then let that memory or picture or image fade from consciousness so that it leaves a sense of warmth, love, and kindness in our heart. With practice, this deepens.

2 We begin to expand this loving kindness toward ourselves, our whole existence. With practice, we will begin to feel warmth, contentment, and love throughout our cells.

3 Then we direct this love to those we love. They might include friends and family as well as people that we do not know but for whom we have tremendous respect, gratitude, and appreciation.

Showing kindness
What emerges out of our heart finds its way into daily life. We can cultivate loving kindness, deep friendship toward friends, strangers and the unfriendly.

4 We visualize strangers—people whom we barely know and with whom we have little association. We might visualize crowd scenes or certain individuals. We allow the warmth and the love to begin to pervade those pictures and images of strangers with whom we may never have the opportunity to have any personal sense of association.

5 Finally, we develop loving kindness and extend it to people whom we do not like. These people might include people who dislike us. We might direct loving kindness to those who engage in acts of violence. These practices are practices to help overcome anger, negativity, hatred, and thoughts of revenge. It is a way of practicing to learn to be clear and accommodating in the face of difficult and distressing circumstances. The regularity of these perceptions of loving kindness can benefit all, as well as our inner life.

When we are hurt, angry, or wrathful, we suffer. It is a way of saying that we still allow others to have a grip over our inner life. To express clarity and love in the face of troublesome circumstances is to rise above the situations and therefore to rise above the limitations of others as much as our own.

There are many occasions when we have a brief exchange with a person or group. Before or after the meeting, we might extend warm and kind thoughts to them:

- *May you be happy*
- *May you be free from pain*
- *May you live in peace.*

life. We can make up our own prayers, chants, or lines which we feel keep our heart open, connected, and receptive. For example:

When we have developed our practice of loving kindness toward loved ones, strangers, and the unfriendly, we can also expand this meditation until it becomes a steady way of being from one day to the next. We might remind ourselves to name in our meditations important people in our

- *May my teachers, community, loved ones, friends, and contacts be free from suffering and pain*
- *May animals and creatures of the Earth, on the ground, in the air, and under water live in safety and security*
- *May my daily activities contribute to the contentment, healing, and insight of others*

If we carry that perception of loving kindness into our interactions with others, it will significantly benefit our relationship with them. We open our heart to give love to loved ones, strangers, and the unfriendly.

Keeping a Journal

MILLIONS OF PEOPLE regularly keep a journal. We often use a journal to record what we did and whom we met on a particular day. Keeping a journal for meditation purposes has a different objective. The primary intention is staying in touch with the inner life. People and places rank secondary to the inner experience. The journal serves as a way to track ourselves, to record our feelings, thoughts, and experiences. We keep in mind what we learn from the day. We record our relationship to the ordinary moments of daily life and the significant periods.

Keeping a journal
A journal will help you to stay in touch with your inner life.

Expanding

the Heart,

Awakening

t h e

M i n d

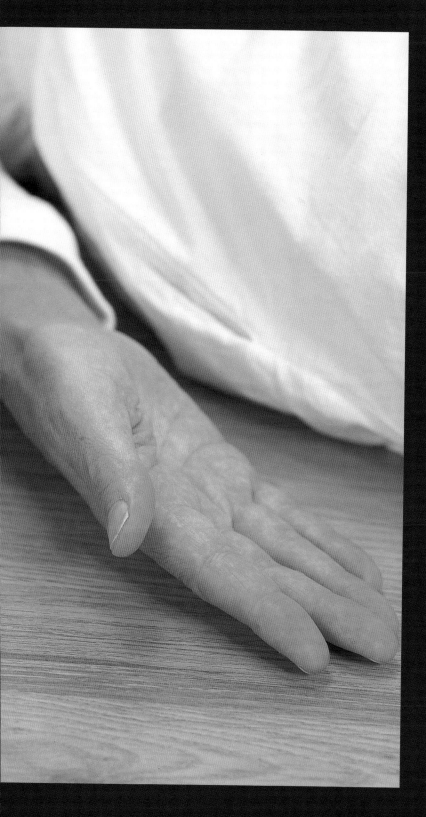

The Mudra of Touching the Elements is performed in the reclining posture. We feel moment to moment our connection with the elements of earth, water, heat, and air.

Meditation not only directs us to a warm heart and clear mind, but also to a depth of awareness of what it means to realize a liberated and enlightened life in daily circumstances. We must not lose sight of the fact that meditation belongs to a comprehensive body of teachings embracing ethics, inquiry, compassion, and wisdom.

AS WE DEVELOP our meditation practice, we might find ourselves naturally looking into every area of our life. We may experience a wish to integrate our regular meditation practice with our deeper values and activities of body, speech, and mind. Meditation develops love for mindful and conscious living with respect for the countless features of daily life.

One of the key words in worthwhile spiritual teachings is practice. Practice covers a wide range of areas. We do not have to confine practice to one or two areas such as stress reduction or healing. If we do, we may forget that we have the potential to awaken every area of our life. It is up to us to reflect on how far we wish to take our meditation practice.

Joy
Practice is to expand every area of our life to allow joy and happiness to flow.

Open your life
*Sitting in meditation with our
hands facing upward, we open our
lives to the fullness of things.*

What is Practice?

- *Practice is for freeing the body
  of destructive patterns, habits,
  and acts of carelessness*
- *Practice is for freeing the mind
  from greed, hate, and confusion*
- *Practice is for cultivating inner
  awareness, to discover depths of
  meditation and to realize
  psychological and spiritual
  insights into the nature of
  things*
- *Practice is the active work of
  the individual transforming
  herself or himself, alone or with
  others*
- *Practice includes equally the
  social, religious, and political
  features of existence. We
  influence the world by our
  practice with the willingness to
  challenge abuse of power*

- *Practice includes working with
  various challenges so that all
  experiences and situations
  belong to practice. At times,
  struggle is an essential factor
  of practice*
- *Theory without practice is
  irresponsible. Practice without
  reason is blind. The route of
  practice is awareness,
  experience, and application*

- *Practice is the starting point for
  insight and awakening. In
  practice, awakened knowledge
  manifests as purposeful activity
  for the welfare of others*
- *Practice is translating living
  perception into a resolute
  awareness, compassionate
  action, transcendent seeing,
  and liberation.*

Ten Areas for Inquiry

Here is a list of some areas for inquiry that can contribute significantly to the deepening of our meditations and understanding of daily life:

1 To reject any livelihood that is threatening or destructive to people, animals, or environment, and to create useful and sustainable activities. The Buddhist tradition emphasizes the importance of right livelihood rather than career.

2 To abide with moderation in life-style and to make possessions last. This requires a degree of mindfulness, and demonstrates care for all material things.

3 To be clear about the number of hours we spend weekly facing a screen, whether it is a television, computer, or movie house. We must watch for patterns of desire, anger, boredom, and restlessness.

4 We make a strong intention and commitment to work on ourselves. This includes the spiritual, emotional, intellectual, and physical aspects, as well as how we relate with others. Wisdom is the willingness to put aside that which is unhealthy for the mind, and to concentrate on practices that are nourishing and insightful.

5 In daily life, we often find ourselves in situations where we need to be respectful to agreements. If we say "yes," "no," or "I will let you know," it is important that we mean it. We practice to honor agreements we have made with others. If we neglect this area, we might find judging others, defending ourselves, or trying to cover up our behavior consumes our meditations.

6 We can experience contact with like-minded people through community, friends, meetings, pilgrimages, and retreats. There is a great deal of kindness and wisdom to be found in the hearts and minds of others through such association. There are people who have much experience in the practice of meditation from whom we can learn a great deal.

Give to those in need
*To give is the heart's confirmation
of connection with those in need.*

9 If we begin to sit regularly
in meditation, we will notice
views, opinions,
standpoints, beliefs, and
ideologies arising and
dissolving in our mind. We
can then become aware of
what influences contribute
to the arising of suffering
and what resolves it.

7 To appreciate and enjoy: being over having, sharing
over taking, letting go over grabbing hold of, and
openness over withdrawal. We can definitely
experience this shift taking place in us, and discover
an expansive understanding of the way things are.

8 We learn to appreciate the importance of giving
support through our service or money, or both, to
the wide range of individuals, charities, and
organizations expressing wisdom and compassion.

10 We can be receptive and
thankful to the many joys of
life through meditation,
contact with others, nature,
creativity, the arts,
awareness, insight, and
freedom. We have the
opportunity to celebrate the
wonders and mysteries of
life. In many respects,
meditation is indispensable
to a full, well-balanced and
emancipated way of being.

Tears and Raindrops —a poem

HEAR this song of our physical
  selves,
Dwell where our body speaks
  quietly of itself.
None can settle apart even with
  what we know.

COMMON link of our participation
  in a green world,
Where intimacy trusts the
  everyday imperative,
And joy is the signal of this
  meeting place.

THIS uncombed hair of the head
  grows
Like the wild grasses of this
  round world.

THIS body lies on its side with
Undulating contours of hills and
  valleys.

LONG, deep breaths flow in and
  out
Like the wind flowing along the
  edges of the moor.

THE blood winds along veins and
  arteries,
As the streams and rivers in soft
  countryside.

WITH eyelids that close on rolling
  plains,
And reveal the darkness of the
  night.

HEAR the occasional sneeze that
  storms
Across the Earth like a hurricane,
And daylight is turned into
  night.

AND the hard bones and joints,
Knuckles and elbows, are but
Rocks and tors of granite
  existence.

THIS benediction bestows
A revelation of harmony,
When all is revealed,
When "I" is forgotten,

AND in the dampness of the
  pounding body,
Where sweat pours across this
  land,
Like the damp mists of sublime
  nature.

FROM time to time,
Tears well up and flow
As a dramatic happening,
Like large raindrops of a
  summer's storm.

PATCHES and growth of clustered
  hair,
Like copses amidst unwoven
  plains.
As human life speaks not only of
  itself.

WORDS emerge out of this blood
  remembering,
Home dwells not where the heart is
But deep in this landscape,
Where there is no measurement.

HEAR THIS SONG OF OURSELVES.

Ethics

WE MUST NOT lose sight of
the fact that meditation
belongs to a comprehensive
body of teachings including
ethics and wisdom. The
core ethic is to refrain
from harming others or
ourselves through actions
of body, speech, and mind.
Buddhists have divided
this ethic into five areas
for reflection.

The practitioner
undertakes the practice to:

- *Restrain from killing*
- *Restrain from stealing*
- *Restrain from causing sexual harm*
- *Restrain from lying*
- *Restrain from abuse of alcohol or drugs.*

At various times, we
can be challenged in any
one or more of these areas.
Our clarity and integrity
suffer when we ignore
respect for any of them.
All five are worth
meditating on. We show
disrespect and create
suffering for ourselves and
others when we:

- *Condone killing*
- *Go for what we want regardless of the harm we cause*
- *Abuse another for sex*
- *Speak without regard for facts or feelings*
- *Distort the balance of our mind through intoxicants.*

Stop suffering
In meditation, we place our hand forward to remind us of the importance of stopping actions that cause suffering from within.

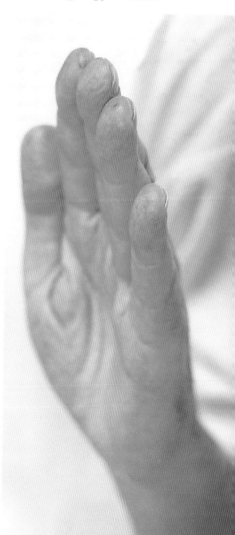

Meditation—an overview

MEDITATION MAKES A substantial contribution to an awakened life. Through meditation we may become exposed to a wide variety of spiritual experiences of which we may or may not be able to make sense. Some meditators like to place these experiences into a religious form of language and some like to leave descriptions out altogether. It is not always easy to tell whether an unusual experience is deep and profound, or simply a passing event in consciousness. What matters is not necessarily the quality of the experience itself, but the understanding that emerges out of it.

Although the experience itself will fade away, it does not mean to say the benefit from the experience also fades. Certain experiences change the direction of our life or give deep renewal and support for dedicated action. Our meditation practices, including working with difficulties and inner transformation, contribute to enlightening our life. There is much for us to discover and realize about our life in this world. Our heart and mind act as a wonderful resource for clarity and understanding. Meditation enables us to discover the full potential of our inner life and to live with integrity, happiness, and creative expression. It is the totality of our daily life that shows how deep our inner transformation.

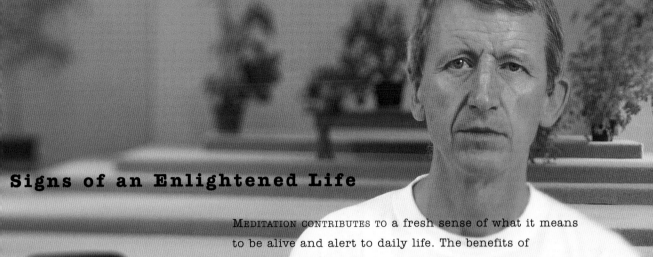

Signs of an Enlightened Life

MEDITATION CONTRIBUTES TO a fresh sense of what it means to be alive and alert to daily life. The benefits of meditation help us find genuine fulfillment as a human being, and the regular practice of meditation sheds light on enlightenment. This includes:

- *Realization of the Immeasurable Truth that embraces diversity and unity, sameness and evolution, relativity and absolutism*
- *A heart filled with deep friendship and love for all*
- *Understanding the conditions for suffering*
- *Respect and application of teachings that honor ethics, meditation, and wisdom*
- *Daily experience of a free mind and generosity of spirit*
- *Happiness, kindness, humor, and noticeable absence of suffering.*

May all beings live with awareness

May all beings live with insight

May all beings realize an enlightened life

For Further Information

IF YOU WISH to explore meditation teachings and practices further, then write to Gaia House for information about our meditation retreat programs running throughout the year. We also publish a newsletter twice a year with news, views, and addresses of our sister centers worldwide. Gaia House has a tape library of around two thousand taped talks on meditation, daily life issues, and associated teachings of internationally respected teachers.

Gaia House
West Ogwell
Newton Abbott
Devon, TQ12 6EN
England
tel: 44 (0)1626 333613
fax: 44 (0)1626 352650
e-mail: gaiahouse@gn.apc.org
website:
http://www.gn.apc.org/gaia house

FOR INFORMATION ABOUT RETREATS IN THE USA WRITE TO:

Insight Meditation Society (IMS)
1230 Pleasant Street,
Barre,
MA 01005.
tel: 508 355 4378
fax: 508 355 6398
Co-founders: Joseph Goldstein, Sharon Salzberg

Spirit Rock Meditation Center
PO Box 909,
Woodacre,
CA 94973.
tel: 415 488 0164
fax: 415 488 0170
Teachers: Jack Kornfield, James Baraz, Sylvia Boorstein, Guy Armstrong

Cambridge Insight Meditation Center
331 Broadway,
Cambridge,
MA 02139.
tel: 617 491 5070
Teachers: Larry Rosenberg, Narayan Liebensen

Taped talks, guided meditations, and e-mail

IT IS MY WISH that the teachings and practices in The
Power of Meditation provide considerable benefit for you
in your daily life. As you engage in your meditations,
you may find questions arising. I would like to give
further support to your inner work. For this I have
asked some senior practitioners of meditation to give
you support through e-mail. You will have the
opportunity to e-mail them with your questions and any
points needing clarification. You may also consider
meditating with others in your area, and exploring
together some of the themes examined in this book. For
further information, please write or e-mail to:

Insight Books (Totnes)

c/o Gaia House.

e-mail:

insightmeditation@gn.apc.org

website:

http://www/insightmeditation.org

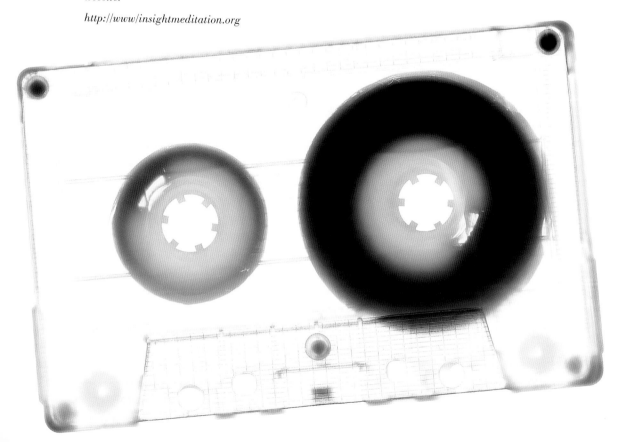

Index

Page numbers in italics refer to illustrations

Acknowledgments

I WISH TO express gratitude to the Buddha, who recognized through his own experience the immense significance of meditation for humanity. From the time of his enlightenment in meditation under the Bodhi Tree in Bodh Gaya, India, he spoke tirelessly about the importance of awareness, meditation, and a fully awakened life. The teachings of the Buddha continue to be a great source of inspiration.

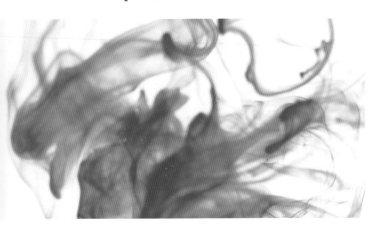

I offer appreciation to Venerable Ajahn Dhammadharo (1914–), of Wat Sai Ngam (Monastery of Beautiful Banyan Trees), Supanburi, Thailand, and a foremost teacher of Insight (Vipassana) Meditation. I spent more than half of my six years as a Buddhist monk in his monastery. Day in and day out, I practised meditation-sitting, walking, standing, and reclining-under his guidance.

Venerable Ajahn Buddhadasa (1907–93) of Wat Suanmoke (Monastery of the Garden of Liberation), Chai Ya, Sura Thani, Thailand, gave me profound teachings and practices, known as the Dharma in the Buddhist tradition. I found his teachings eminently suitable for daily life circumstances.

My gratitude also goes to Sharda Rogell and Gill Farrer-Halls for editing The Power of Meditation. Sharda teaches retreats with me worldwide. Gill has practiced meditation for many years and understands the importance of it for a wise and compassionate life. Their suggestions were invaluable.

Thanks to Marnie Haslam, Elizabeth Healey, Rebecca Moy, Michelle Pickering, and Hilary Sagar of Quarto Publishing for their cooperation and advice in the writing of this book.

I also wish to thank N'shorna, my daughter, for her ongoing support and lovely presence, my mother, late father, and Gwanwyn Williams. Finally, thank you to everybody connected with Gaia House, our retreat center in South Devon, England.

I hope The Power of Meditation will make a wonderful contribution to a fully awakened life for all readers, whether you meditate alone, in small groups, or both. May your lives be rich in joy and and understanding.

May all beings live in peace
May all beings live in harmony
May all beings be fully enlightened